Conference Proceedings of the Society for Experimental Mechanics Series

Series Editor

Kristin B. Zimmerman
Society for Experimental Mechanics, Inc.,
Bethel, USA

The Conference Proceedings of the Society for Experimental Mechanics Series presents early findings and case studies from a wide range of fundamental and applied work across the broad range of fields that comprise Experimental Mechanics. Series volumes follow the principle tracks or focus topics featured in each of the Society's two annual conferences: IMAC, A Conference and Exposition on Structural Dynamics, and the Society's Annual Conference & Exposition and will address critical areas of interest to researchers and design engineers working in all areas of Structural Dynamics, Solid Mechanics and Materials Research.

Thomas Matarazzo • François Hemez • Eleonora Maria Tronci • Austin Downey
Editors

Data Science in Engineering, Vol. 11

Proceedings of the 43rd IMAC, A Conference and Exposition on Structural Dynamics 2025

River Publishers

Published, sold and distributed by:

River Publishers
Broagervej 10
9260 Gistrup
Denmark

www.riverpublishers.com

ISBN 97887-438-0156-6 (Hardback)

ISBN 97887-438-0168-9 (eBook)

https://doi.org/10.13052/9788743801566

Conference Proceedings of the Society for Experimental Mechanics

An imprint of River Publishers

Preface

Data Science in Engineering represents one of twelve volumes of technical papers presented at the 43rd IMAC, A Conference and Exposition on Structural Dynamics, organized by the Society for Experimental Mechanics, and held February 10-13, 2025. The full proceedings also include volumes on Nonlinear Structures & Systems; Dynamics of Civil Structures; Model Validation and Uncertainty Quantification; Dynamic Substructuring & Transfer Path Analysis; Special Topics in Structural Dynamics & Experimental Techniques; Computer Vision & Laser Vibrometry; Dynamic Environments Testing; Sensors & Instrumentation and Aircraft/Aerospace Testing Techniques; and Topics in Modal Analysis & Parameter Identification I & II; and Structural health Monitoring & Machine Learning.

The Data Science in Engineering technical division of the Society for Experimental Mechanics focuses on the transformative role and application of data analytics and modeling in structural, aerospace and mechanical engineering. With the rapid advancements in sensing technologies (high-speed cameras, image processing, laser sensors, unmanned aerial vehicles, etc.) and high-performance computing, engineering systems now generate vast volumes of data that demand advanced analytical frameworks to manage big data and extract useful information. Machine learning, deep learning, transfer learning, big data, statistics, and related methods define the analytical toolset to process vast volumes of measurements and predictions, analyze complex phenomena, identify trends and relationships, and guide the development of predictive models through data. Statistical and machine learning methods provide fast, robust, adaptive, and scalable solutions for the online monitoring of structures and mechanical systems, and to support decision-making and risk analysis. These advancements are transforming how engineers collect and process data, shifting from reactive assessments to proactive strategies that enhance system understanding, performance, resilience and operational efficiency.

The organizers would like to thank the authors, presenters, session organizers, and session chairs for their participation in this track.

Editors
Thomas Matarazzo–*United States Military Academy*; François Hemez, *Lawrence Livermore National Laboratory,* Livermore, CA, USA; Eleonora Maria Tronci–*Northeastern University;* Austin Downey – *University of South Carolina*

Contents

Chapter 1
Data-Driven Method for Reduced Order Modeling of Blisks with Large and Small Mistuning

Mihai Cimpuieru, Sean T. Kelly, and Bogdan I. Epureanu

Abstract Turbomachinery blisks are paramount to the safe and efficient operation of gas turbines. They are exposed to large aerodynamic forces while functioning at extreme temperatures and rotating conditions. In addition, blisks are manufactured as one single piece and have low damping, making them susceptible to large vibrations, which are amplified by inherent blisk mistuning, represented by small differences from the nominal design. Furthermore, vibration responses are drastically affected by large mistuning (e.g., cracked or deformed blades) in one or more sectors of the blisk, called rogue sectors. These properties make blisks susceptible to high cycle fatigue, which can result in failure of the structure. Thus, it is essential to predict responses of mistuned blisks with rogue sectors. Tuned blisk responses can be calculated at a low computational cost. However, mistuning and rogue blades break the cyclicity of the system and make response calculations much more challenging. State-of-the-art computational methods address this challenge by using reduced-order models (ROMs) based on tuned modes of cyclic rogue systems. However, computing these ROMs requires formulating one or more sets of full system matrices, which can be computationally expensive. To address this issue, one method developed by the authors utilizes a data-driven approach that enforces known physics derived from equations of motion. Nevertheless, this existing method cannot be applied to blisks with rogue sectors. This manuscript proposes an extension of the state-of-the-art to compute responses of a mistuned blisk with rogue sectors. This approach uses transfer function matrices from both a rogue blisk and pristine blisk to form a linear system of equations to compute blade responses, and is applicable to cases including multiple rogue sectors of various types. This approach is demonstrated for a lumped mass model with 18 blades with one or more rogue sectors. Results show that this method can predict amplitude responses of mistuned blisks with rogue sectors with absolute percent errors below 8%.

Keywords Turbomachinery · Neural Networks · Structural Dynamics · Data Science · Machine Learning

Introduction

Gas turbines are one of the most widely used propulsion systems due to their high power and efficiency. Turbomachinery blisks are often used in the compressor and turbine stages of these systems, interacting with the passing air flow and operating at extreme conditions. Gas turbine efficiency and safety are highly dependent on the air flow-blisk interaction. Hence, it is paramount to understand and continuously develop the state-of-the-art for modeling turbomachinery blisks to ensure efficient and safe operation. These structures are exposed to high aerodynamic forces, are manufactured as one single piece, and have low damping, all of which can result in high amplitude blade vibrations. In addition, as-manufactured blisks are mistuned, i.e., contain small deviations from nominal material properties and/or geometry at the blade level. Furthermore, due to significant wear formation or even damage at one or more blades, blisks can also suffer from so-called large mistuning. Blade vibrations due to either or both of these phenomena can result in high cycle fatigue, causing failure of the structure and potentially disastrous effects on the operational safety of a gas turbine. Hence, it is paramount to predict blisk responses with both small and large mistuning. For a tuned blisk (i.e., no mistuning), the computational effort to compute the blisk response can be highly reduced by leveraging the cyclic-symmetry of the structure using block circulant system matrices and projections onto cyclic coordinates. However, mistuning breaks the cyclic-symmetry of the structure. Thus, one cannot directly leverage the tuned system's cyclic symmetry for reduction, resulting in increased total computational effort.

Mihai Cimpuieru · Sean T. Kelly · Bogdan I. Epureanu
University of Michigan, Ann Arbor, MI 48103
e-mail: mcimpi@umich.edu; seantk@umich.edu; epureanu@umich.edu

Thomas Matarazzo et al. (eds.), *Data Science in Engineering, Vol. 11*, Conference Proceedings of the Society for Experimental Mechanics Series, https://doi.org/10.13052/9788743801566-1

Thus, formulating reduced-order models (ROMs) to compute mistuned blisk responses has been of great interest in the past decades.

There are several state-of-the-art ROMs to compute mistuned blisk responses. Firstly, small mistuning is commonly defined in literature as small deviations in the cantilever blade alone frequencies with no change in the blade mode shape. Computationally, small mistuning is modeled by stochastically varying the blade's Young's modulus from blade to blade, usually no more than 5% [1]. Multiple ROMs have been developed using physics-based approaches, such as component mode synthesis (CMS) techniques [2]. These methods separately consider the blades and disk sections, utilizing interface constraint modes and normal modes of each section holding the interface between the two sections fixed. Other physics-based ROMs consider a subset of or all the tuned blisk modes when blades are exhibiting cantilever beam motion, while some also include constraint modes associated with the disk-blade interface [3,4]. Secondly, for large mistuning, some methods build upon a CMS-based approach by structuring the mistuned blisk into a tuned blisk component and a mistuned blisk component. However, these substructuring-based approaches require one or more sets of large full-order system matrices. Other approaches have focused on leveraging the cyclic-symmetry of tuned systems [5]. In particular, the pristine-rogue-interface modal expansion (PRIME) method [6,7] uses a basis formed from modes of the tuned system with pristine blades and modes of a tuned system with rogue blades (i.e., all blisk blades have the same large mistuning). Additionally, using an extension of [3], PRIME can predict blisk responses with both small and large mistuning.

A primary drawback of physics-based ROMs is that they require the use of high dimensional blisk finite element (FE) models to characterize the system dynamics and build the projection bases used for ROM generation. Furthermore, the accuracy of a physics-based ROM cannot be enhanced using experimental data. Hence, recent work has focused on the development of data-driven methods to predict the response of mistuned blisks [8,9]. In particular, for small mistuning, some methods leverage feedforward neural networks (FFNNs) and a combination of coupling and sector-response networks to predict blade tip responses [9]. Specifically, the method in Ref. [9] uses a sector-level coupling FFNN to predict the responses at sector interfaces while enforcing compatibility conditions, and then uses those responses as input for a separate sector-level FFNN to compute the tip response for each blade. However, this method does not explicitly enforce the system linearity (and hence the governing physics) in the networks nor the solution procedure. As such, a new method to account for this drawback was developed [10,11]. Specifically, this method leverages the cyclic-nature of blisks and enforces system linearity within the loss function of a sector-level, physics-informed neural network (PINN). In particular, this approach introduces two matrix transfer functions: one that relates sector i blade responses to potentially all other blade responses, and one that relates the same sector i blade responses to the forcing applied on sector i. These transfer function matrices are output from the sector-level PINN for each sector and used to form a linear system of equations to predict all blade responses. However, this approach accounts only for small mistuning, without considering large changes in mode shape due to large changes in material properties or geometry. To the authors' knowledge, there is currently no physics-informed data-driven method for predicting blisk responses with both small and large mistuning.

This paper proposes a novel physics-informed data-driven method to compute the response of blisks with both small and large mistuning. Conceptually similar to the PRIME method, the authors utilize two cyclic systems: 1) a pristine blisk with small mistuning, and 2) a rogue blisk with small mistuning. Two sets of sector-level transfer function matrices relating the blade root responses of a sector i to 1) the blade root responses of all other blades and 2) the forcing excitation on sector i are learned. Specifically, one set is learned by a sector-level PINN trained using the cyclic pristine blisk with small mistuning, and the other set is learned by a separate sector-level PINN trained using the cyclic rogue blisk with small mistuning. These two sets of sector-level transfer function matrices are then used to form a linear system of equations that is solved to predict all blade root responses of a blisk with small mistuning and rogue blades. The blisk blade tip responses can then be predicted using the computed blade root responses in a similar manner to that used in Ref. [9]. Prediction results considering a traveling-wave excitation (TWE) with fixed amplitude and a blisk with small mistuning and 1, 2, or 17 rogue blades are presented. Across all presented results, this method predicts blade root responses with absolute percent errors less than 8%.

Methodology

The goal of this approach is to predict blisk responses at the blade roots when one or more blades are rogue (i.e., have large mistuning) and all blades have small mistuning. For this analysis, we will consider that all rogue blades have the same amount of large mistuning. However, this method can be applied to blisks with multiple blades with varying levels of "rogueness".

Firstly, it is critical to define the neural networks used throughout this paper. Two sector-level PINNs (similar to those in [10, 11]]) with 2 fully-connected hidden layers each having 500 nodes are utilized for this work. For a general sector i, each network takes as input the small blade mistuning of sector i, denoted δ_i, and the TWE frequency, ω. The output of each network consists of two matrices, $\mathbf{A}(\omega, \delta_i)$ and $\mathbf{B}(\omega, \delta_i)$, defined as transfer function matrices respectively describing the relationship of the sector i blade root responses to 1) all other blade root responses, and 2) the forcing applied to blade i (see Eq. (1)). In Eq. (1), $\overline{x}_{i,\omega}$ are the blade root responses of sector i for excitation frequency ω, $\overline{f}_{i,\omega}$ is the force applied at the blade tip of sector i, and $\overline{x}_{\neg i,\omega}$ are the blade root responses from all sectors except sector i. The mean squared error (MSE) loss function for a single training sample is defined in Eq. (2), the goal being to learn the optimal $\mathbf{A}(\omega, \delta_i)$ and $\mathbf{B}(\omega, \delta_i)$ that minimize the overall MSE across all training samples. Note that a factor of $1/2n$ is included in Eq. (2). This comes from using n blade root responses per sector, with 2 included in the denominator because, for PINN training, real and imaginary responses are explicitly considered in $\overline{x}_{i,\omega}$ and $\overline{x}_{\neg i,\omega}$ rather than as combined complex-value quantities.

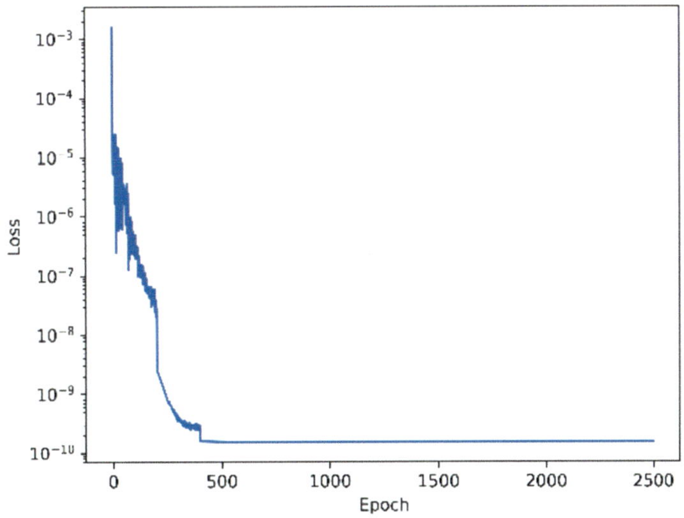

Fig. 1 Loss function during training of pristine blisk PINN.

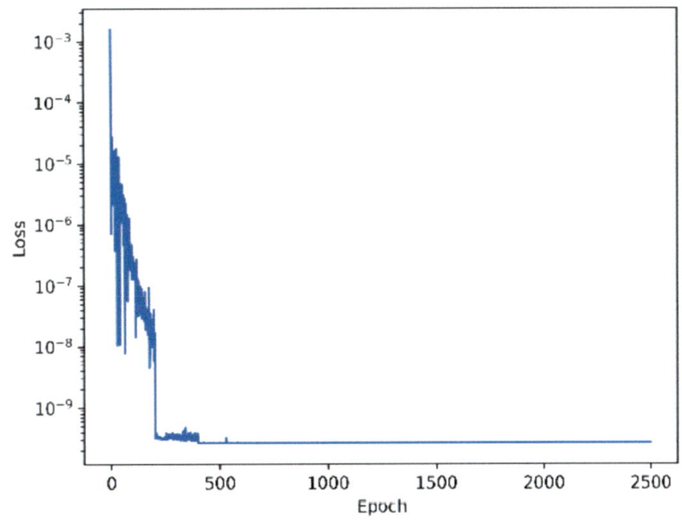

Fig. 2 Loss function during training of rogue blisk PINN.

The sector-level formulation in Eq. (1) leverages the cyclicity of the blisk and is explained in more detail in Refs. [10,11]. However, it is important to mention that the PINNs in [10,11] take as inputs the mistuning values of all or of a subset of the other blades since all responses are measured at the tip of the blades where the responses are significantly affected by mistuning. The formulation the authors propose in this work utilizes responses only from the blade roots. Note that the response of blade i at its root is only dependent on 1) the mistuning of blade i since the force is applied at its tip, and 2) the root responses of all other blades due to coupling through the disk section. Thus, the input to the network proposed here only consists of 1) the excitation frequency, and 2) the mistuning of the sector i. The network is trained for a frequency range 940 Hz – 1060 Hz, with a frequency resolution of 0.3 Hz. Training is performed using a total of 577,440 individual samples.

Secondly, it is important to clarify what systems are considered for the proposed method. As mentioned in the previous section, there will be two systems analyzed, each with a respective PINN: 1) a blisk with pristine blades (i.e., no large mistuning) and small mistuning, and 2) a blisk with rogue blades and small mistuning, each blade having the same level of "rogueness" (i.e., same large mistuning applied at each blade). The respective PINN training curves (i.e., overall MSE loss vs. epoch) are shown in Figs. 1 and 2. For both networks, the learning rate is reduced in 200-epoch increments to reach convergence faster. The training curves in Figs. 1 and 2 show that both networks converge successfully.

Next, a linear system of equations is formed combining the $\mathbf{A}(\omega, \delta_i)$ and $\mathbf{B}(\omega, \delta_i)$ matrices obtained from the two PINNs as presented in Eq. (3). Blade root response predictions for a blisk with both pristine and rogue sectors are obtained by solving the linear system in Eq. (3), where to predict sector i blade root responses and, for example, considering rogue blisk coefficients, we have $\mathbf{A}(\omega, \delta_i)_R = \left[\mathbf{A}(\omega, \delta_i)_R^1\ \mathbf{A}(\omega, \delta_i)_R^2 \ldots \mathbf{A}(\omega, \delta_i)_R^{i-1}\ \mathbf{A}(\omega, \delta_i)_R^{i+1} \ldots \mathbf{A}(\omega, \delta_i)_R^{17}\ \mathbf{A}(\omega, \delta_i)_R^{18}\right]$ with $\mathbf{A}(\omega, \delta_i)_R^j$ being the sector j blade root response coefficients used to predict sector i's blade root response when blade i is rogue. Similarly, the same definition applies for pristine sectors. Within this system of equations, for rogue blades we use the $\mathbf{A}(\omega, \delta_i)$ and $\mathbf{B}(\omega, \delta_i)$ matrices output from the rogue blisk PINN, while for pristine blades we use the matrices output from the pristine blisk PINN. In Eq. (3), blades i and $i+1$ are selected to be rogue to exemplify how the blade "rogueness" is taken into account in the mathematical formulation using the learned transfer function matrices. These specific equations are boxed in Eq. (3).

$$\overline{x}_{i,\omega} = \begin{bmatrix} \mathbf{A}(\omega, \delta_i) & \mathbf{B}(\omega, \delta_i) \end{bmatrix} \begin{bmatrix} \overline{x}_{\neg i,\omega} \\ \overline{f}_{i,\omega} \end{bmatrix} \tag{1}$$

$$L = \frac{1}{2n} \left\| \overline{x}_{i,\omega} - \begin{bmatrix} \mathbf{A}(\omega, \delta_i) & \mathbf{B}(\omega, \delta_i) \end{bmatrix} \begin{bmatrix} \overline{x}_{\neg i,\omega} \\ \overline{f}_{i,\omega} \end{bmatrix} \right\|_2^2 \tag{2}$$

$$\begin{bmatrix} 0 & \mathbf{A}(\omega,\delta_1)_P^2 & \mathbf{A}(\omega,\delta_1)_P^3 & \cdots & \mathbf{A}(\omega,\delta_1)_P^{16} & \mathbf{A}(\omega,\delta_1)_P^{17} & \mathbf{A}(\omega,\delta_1)_P^{18} \\ \mathbf{A}(\omega,\delta_2)_P^1 & 0 & \mathbf{A}(\omega,\delta_2)_P^3 & \cdots & \mathbf{A}(\omega,\delta_2)_P^{16} & \mathbf{A}(\omega,\delta_2)_P^{17} & \mathbf{A}(\omega,\delta_2)_P^{18} \\ \vdots & \vdots & \vdots & \ddots & \vdots & \vdots & \vdots \\ \mathbf{A}(\omega,\delta_i)_R^1 & \mathbf{A}(\omega,\delta_i)_R^2 & \mathbf{A}(\omega,\delta_i)_R^3 & \cdots & \mathbf{A}(\omega,\delta_i)_R^{16} & \mathbf{A}(\omega,\delta_i)_R^{17} & \mathbf{A}(\omega,\delta_i)_R^{18} \\ \mathbf{A}(\omega,\delta_{i+1})_R^1 & \mathbf{A}(\omega,\delta_{i+1})_R^2 & \mathbf{A}(\omega,\delta_{i+1})_R^3 & \cdots & \mathbf{A}(\omega,\delta_{i+1})_R^{16} & \mathbf{A}(\omega,\delta_{i+1})_R^{17} & \mathbf{A}(\omega,\delta_{i+1})_R^{18} \\ \vdots & \vdots & \vdots & \ddots & \vdots & \vdots & \vdots \\ \mathbf{A}(\omega,\delta_{17})_P^1 & \mathbf{A}(\omega,\delta_{17})_P^2 & \mathbf{A}(\omega,\delta_{17})_P^3 & \cdots & \mathbf{A}(\omega,\delta_{17})_P^{16} & 0 & \mathbf{A}(\omega,\delta_{17})_P^{18} \\ \mathbf{A}(\omega,\delta_{18})_P^1 & \mathbf{A}(\omega,\delta_{18})_P^2 & \mathbf{A}(\omega,\delta_{18})_P^3 & \cdots & \mathbf{A}(\omega,\delta_{18})_P^{16} & \mathbf{A}(\omega,\delta_{18})_P^{17} & 0 \end{bmatrix} \begin{bmatrix} \bar{x}_{1,\omega} \\ \bar{x}_{2,\omega} \\ \vdots \\ \bar{x}_{i,\omega} \\ \bar{x}_{i+1,\omega} \\ \vdots \\ \bar{x}_{17,\omega} \\ \bar{x}_{18,\omega} \end{bmatrix} + \begin{bmatrix} \mathbf{B}(\omega,\delta_1)_P \overline{f}_{1,\omega} \\ \mathbf{B}(\omega,\delta_2)_P \overline{f}_{2,\omega} \\ \vdots \\ \mathbf{B}(\omega,\delta_i)_R \overline{f}_{i,\omega} \\ \mathbf{B}(\omega,\delta_{i+1})_R \overline{f}_{i+1,\omega} \\ \vdots \\ \mathbf{B}(\omega,\delta_{17})_P \overline{f}_{17,\omega} \\ \mathbf{B}(\omega,\delta_{18})_P \overline{f}_{18,\omega} \end{bmatrix} = \begin{bmatrix} \bar{x}_{1,\omega} \\ \bar{x}_{2,\omega} \\ \vdots \\ \bar{x}_{i,\omega} \\ \bar{x}_{i+1,\omega} \\ \vdots \\ \bar{x}_{17,\omega} \\ \bar{x}_{18,\omega} \end{bmatrix} \tag{3}$$

Analysis

To validate this approach, an 18-sector blisk lumped mass model is considered, with a sector-level illustration of this model shown in Fig. 3. Small mistuning is introduced at the blade level by proportionally varying both blade-specific spring constants (i.e., $k_{b_0}^i$ and $k_{b_1}^i$) by the same value. Here, large mistuning (for a rogue blade) is introduced by increasing both of these spring constants by 15%, though other values could be considered to generate large mistuning. A TWE with a vibration amplitude of 1 N is applied to mass $m_{b_2}^i$.

To evaluate this method's ability to predict blisk responses with both small and large mistuning, multiple rogue blisks with different small mistuning patterns were tested. Initially, a blisk with one small mistuning pattern (i.e., 18 small mistuning values, each value applied to one of the blisk blades) and varying number of rogue blades was considered. Small mistuning values are randomly sampled from a normal distribution with 0 mean and 1% standard deviation. Considering the same small mistuning pattern, the following results are obtained for blisks with 1 rogue blade, 2 rogue blades, and 17 rogue blades. It

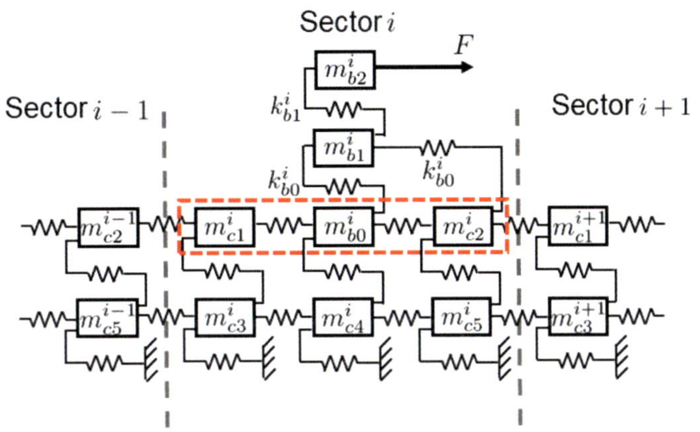

Fig. 3 Blisk lumped mass model – sector level viewpoint.

is important to emphasize that this approach was also tested by the authors for multiple other small mistuning patterns with the number of rogue blades ranging from 1 to 18. However, these tests are not shown in here for brevity.

For all three cases presented (i.e., same small mistuning pattern with 1 rogue blade, 2 rogue blades, and 17 rogue blades), Figs. 4, 5, and 6 show blisk response envelope predictions (i.e., the maximum response across all blades at each excitation frequency) with absolute percent errors all less than 8%. In particular, with only 1 or 2 rogue blades, the envelope response errors are below 6%. Future investigation is needed to better understand the higher errors associated with adding more rogue blades. Figures 7, 8, and 9 show response predictions for each blade root degree of freedom, where the dotted lines are the predicted responses using the proposed approach and the solid lines are the actual (i.e., reference) responses. These results show that this method accurately predicts the actual blade root responses, not only for the maximum values of the responses shown in Figs. 4, 5, and 6, but for all blade responses in the considered frequency range. The blade real and imaginary

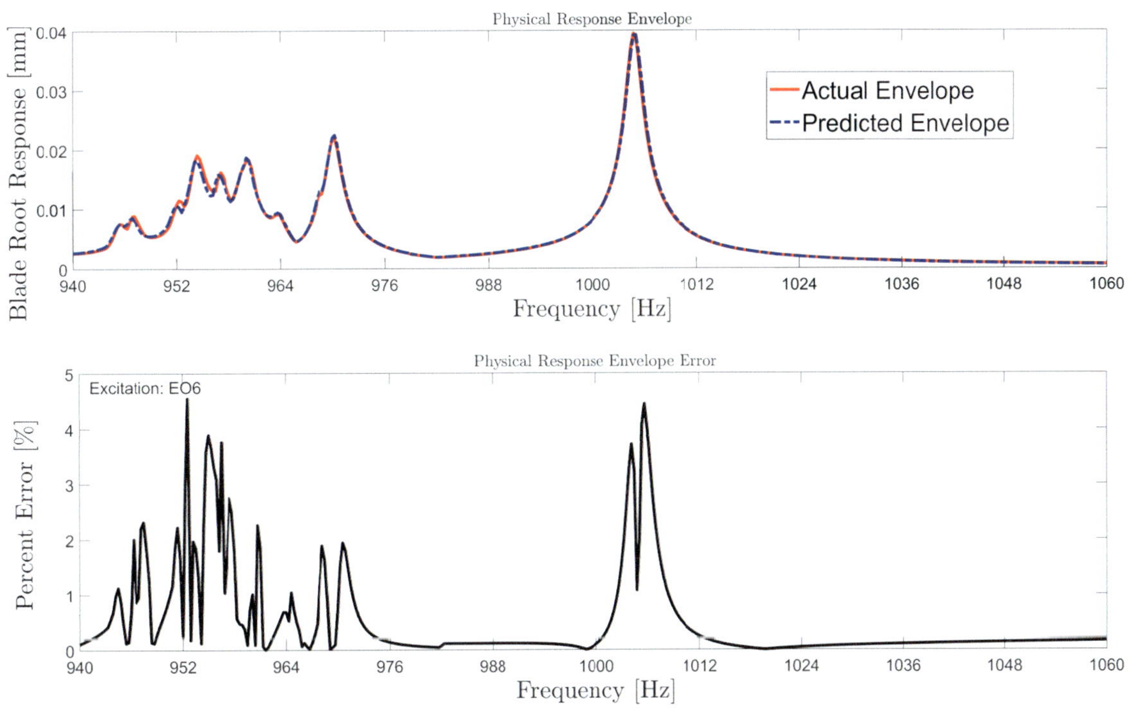

Fig. 4 (Top) Blisk response envelope prediction and (bottom) absolute percent error with small mistuning and 1 rogue blade.

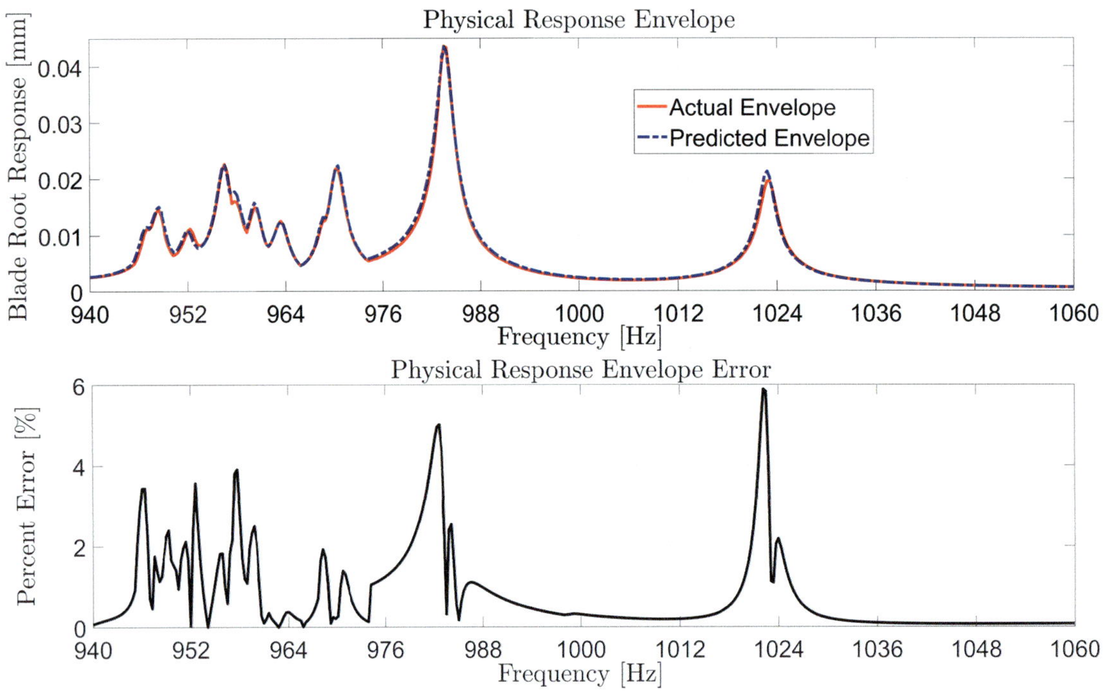

Fig. 5 (Top) Blisk response envelope prediction and (bottom) absolute percent error with small mistuning and 2 rogue blades.

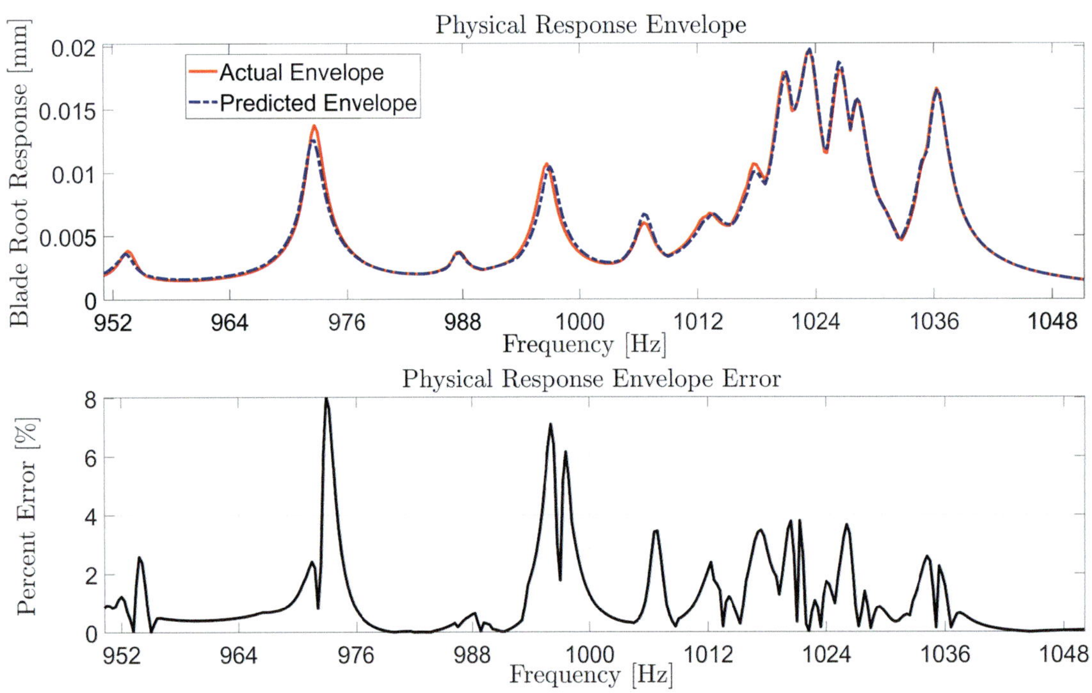

Fig. 6 (Top) Blisk response envelope prediction and (bottom) absolute percent error with small mistuning and 17 rogue blades.

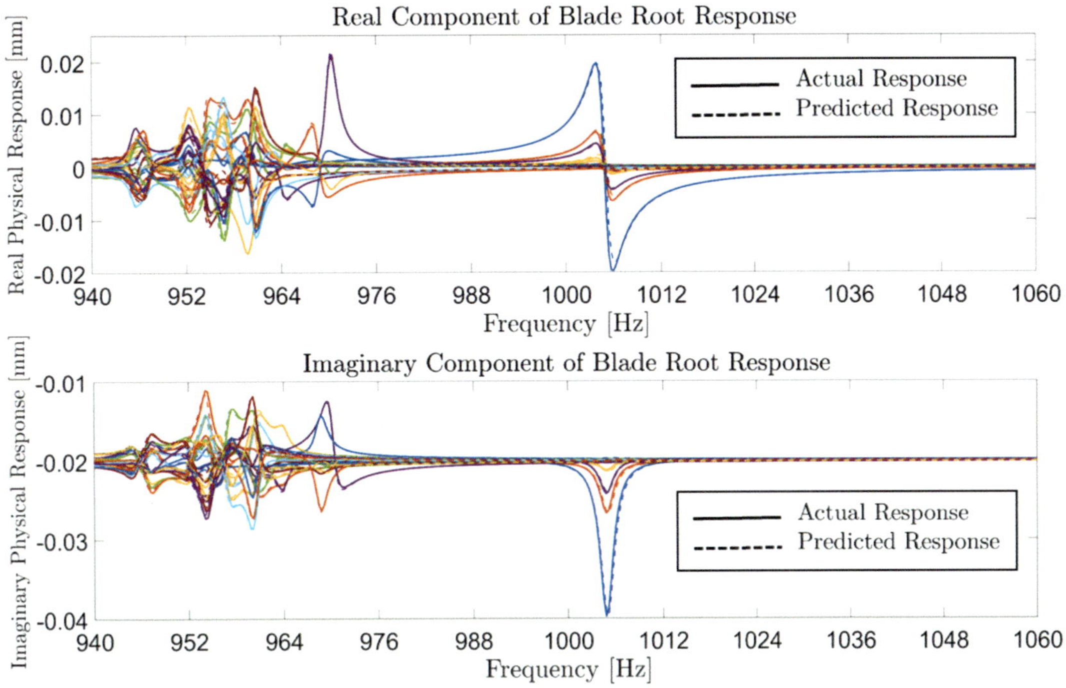

Fig. 7 (Top) Real and (bottom) imaginary blisk response prediction for all blades considering small mistuning and 1 rogue blade.

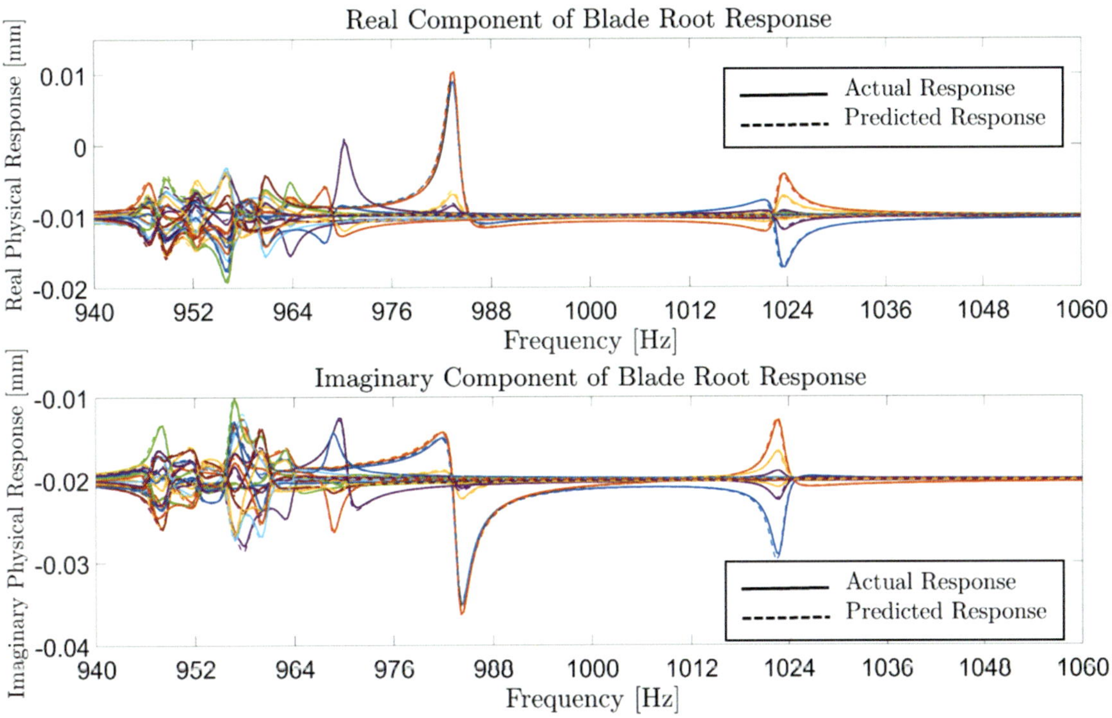

Fig. 8 (Top) Real and (bottom) imaginary blisk response prediction for all blades considering small mistuning and 2 rogue blades.

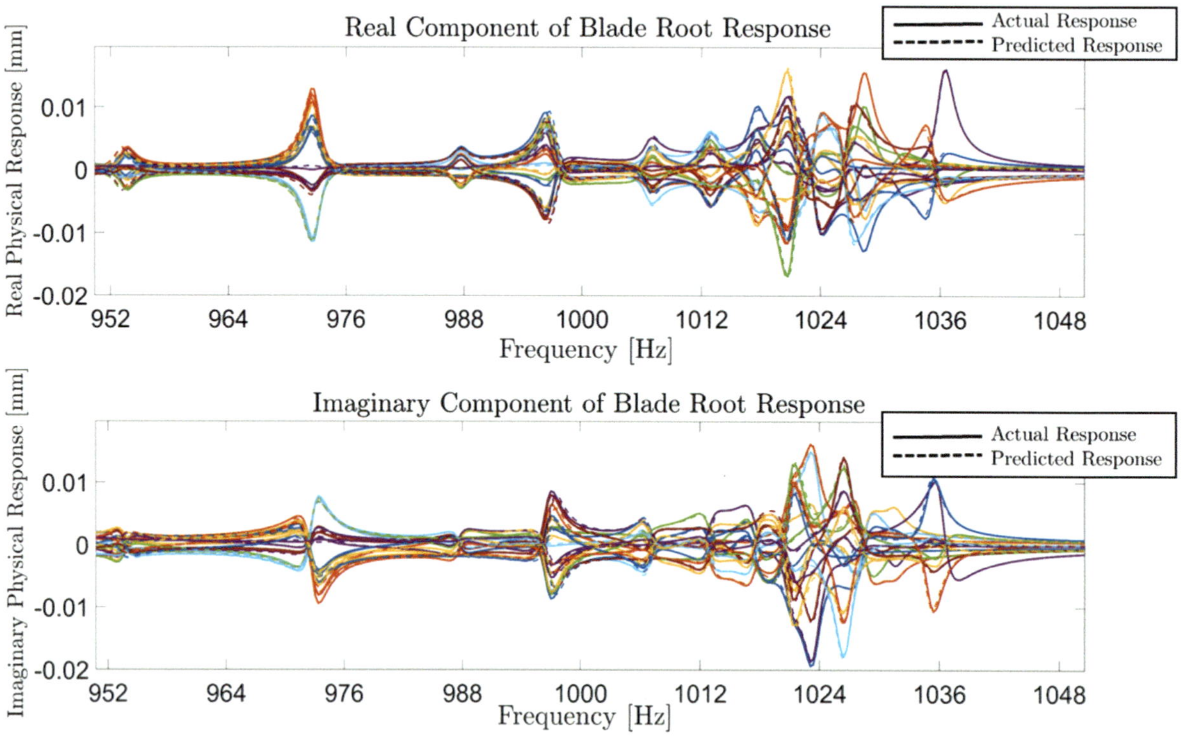

Fig. 9 (Top) Real and (bottom) imaginary blisk response prediction for all blades considering small mistuning and 17 rogue blades.

responses are reported separately because, as stated previously, the response vector $\overline{x}_{i,\omega}$ is split into real and imaginary components for training both PINNs.

Conclusion

To summarize, this paper proposes a physics-informed data-driven reduced-order modeling approach to predict blisk responses with small and large mistuning. This method builds upon a previous technique developed by the authors that leverages the blisk's cyclic properties and enforces system linearity through a sector-level PINN. The proposed method is the first physics informed data driven method able to capture blisk responses with both small and large mistuning. The method combines the transfer function matrices learned for a pristine blisk with small mistuning and a cyclic rogue blisk with small mistuning to predict the blade root responses of a blisk with one or more rogue sectors. The blade root responses can then be used to predict the blade tip response using a previously developed data-driven technique. The presented results show accurate predictions, with absolute percent errors below 8%. Future work includes identifying potential accuracy enhancements through tuning of the network training parameters (e.g., frequency resolution, frequency range, and amplitude normalization).

References

1. Mitra, M., and Epureanu, B. I., 2019, "Dynamic Modeling and Projection-Based Reduction Methods for Bladed Disks With Nonlinear Frictional and Intermittent Contact Interfaces," Applied Mechanics Reviews, **71**(5), p. 050803. https://doi.org/10.1115/1.4043083.
2. Bladh, R., Castanier, M. P., and Pierre, C., 2000, "Component-Mode-Based Reduced Order Modeling Techniques for Mistuned Bladed Disks—Part I: Theoretical Models," Journal of Engineering for Gas Turbines and Power, **123**(1), pp. 89–99. https://doi.org/10.1115/1.1338947.
3. Lim, S.-H., Bladh, R., Castanier, M. P., and Pierre, C., 2007, "Compact, Generalized Component Mode Mistuning Representation for Modeling Bladed Disk Vibration," AIAA Journal, **45**(9), pp. 2285–2298. https://doi.org/10.2514/1.13172.

4. Fitzner, C., Epureanu, B. I., and Filippi, S., 2014, "Nodal Energy Weighted Transformation: A Mistuning Projection and Its Application to FLADE^{TM} Turbines," Mechanical Systems and Signal Processing, **42**(1–2), pp. 167–180. https://doi.org/10.1016/j.ymssp.2013.08.027.
5. Mbaye, M., Soize, C., and Ousty, J.-P., 2010, "A Reduced-Order Model of Detuned Cyclic Dynamical Systems With Geometric Modifications Using a Basis of Cyclic Modes," Journal of Engineering for Gas Turbines and Power, **132**(11), p. 112502. https://doi.org/10.1115/1.4000805.
6. Madden, A., Epureanu, B. I., and Filippi, S., 2012, "Reduced-Order Modeling Approach for Blisks with Large Mass, Stiffness, and Geometric Mistuning," AIAA Journal, **50**(2), pp. 366–374. https://doi.org/10.2514/1.J051140.
7. Tang, W., Epureanu, B. I., and Filippi, S., 2017, "Models for Blisks with Large Blends and Small Mistuning," Mechanical Systems and Signal Processing, **87**, pp. 161–179. https://doi.org/10.1016/j.ymssp.2016.10.019.
8. Fan, Y., Fan, J., Li, A., Wu, Y., Zhang, Y., and Song, Z., 2024, "A Physics-Informed Neural Network Surrogate Model for Mistuned Bladed Disks Dynamics," *Volume 10B: Structures and Dynamics — Fatigue, Fracture, and Life Prediction; Probabilistic Methods; Rotordynamics; Structural Mechanics and Vibration*, American Society of Mechanical Engineers, London, United Kingdom, p. V10BT27A016. https://doi.org/10.1115/GT2024-125397.
9. Kelly, S. T., Lupini, A., and Epureanu, B. I., 2021, "Data-Driven Modeling Approach for Mistuned Cyclic Structures," AIAA Journal, **59**(7), pp. 2684–2696. https://doi.org/10.2514/1.J060117.
10. Kelly, S. T., "Data-Driven Models of Blisk Structures."
11. Kelly, S. T., and Epureanu, B. I., 2024, "Physics-Informed Machine Learning Approach for Reduced – Order Modeling of Integrally Bladed Rotors, Journal of Sound and Vibration – Accepted 2024

Chapter 2
System Identification of Data from Rotating Machinery Using Deep Learning Network Training

R. Wetherington and M. Kasprzyk

Abstract Deep learning algorithms are a powerful tool that can be used in the identification of unique features and behavior of data, yet applying these algorithms in practice can require innovative solutions for different application domains. This paper discusses a simple approach for mapping single-channel data (like that produced by accelerometers and proximity probes) from a rotating machine, , such that it can be used for the training of a simple convolutional neural network. The resulting trained neural network can accurately identify data features to its source with useful accuracy. This method could be used to identify known unique operating system characteristics for prognostic and diagnostic assessment. This paper discusses an evaluation of this approach using real and simulated data, and the results are presented herein.

Keywords AI networks · Neural networks · Rotating machine · Sensor · Mapping data · Diagnostic

Introduction

Developmental testing of rotating machinery can involve dozens of sensor channels and high-speed sampling of the sensor values. Sample rates of tens of thousands of samples per second are not uncommon. The sinusoidal nature of these data present the option of remapping it from 1D to 2D using an X-Y projection method, such as what is used in orbit plots [1]. The projected 2D figures exhibit impressive consistency that are often unique to the source. When the signal-to-noise ratio is high, these signals often present distinguishable features in the data. Therefore, it becomes possible to process the information with a simple convolutional neural network designed for character recognition. The resulting trained AI network can then accurately identify data features to its source to allow insight into the mechanical and design properties that cause the features.

This paper evaluates this approach using data acquired from a six-disc mechanical fault simulator (MFS), as well as from a software-based signal simulator. The MFS sensor data were acquired with a National Instruments data acquisition system and analyzed with MATLAB and its Deep Learning Toolbox,[2]. The trained and validated neural networks were benchmarked with an independent test data set.

Background and Methodology

Dynamic test engineers use orbit plots to analyze the behavior of rotors under operating conditions. They typically do this using a pair of proximity probes placed 90 degrees apart with respect to the rotation axis. Data are digitally acquired at high rates and projected as a scatter plot with the data from one channel projecting along the X-axis and the other channel projecting along the Y-axis. The resulting imagery is interpreted for rotor behavior.

A single axis of sensors are sometimes used to monitor clearances, or general-purpose accelerometers are used for vibration monitoring. In these cases, a secondary set of channels, placed 90 degrees with respect to the first set, is not available. If the rotating article is behaving as a symmetrically mounted rigid body, then a synthesized secondary channel can be approximated from the primary sensor to facilitate the creation of a 2D map. There are two straightforward methods for simulating a second sensor channel positioned 90 degrees from the first sensor.

R. Wetherington · M. Kasprzyk
Oak Ridge National Laboratory, Oak Ridge, TN 37830
e-mail: wetheringtgr@ornl.gov; kasprzykmr@ornl.gov

Thomas Matarazzo et al. (eds.), *Data Science in Engineering, Vol. 11*, Conference Proceedings of the Society for Experimental Mechanics Series, https://doi.org/10.13052/9788743801566-2

The first method is to take the primary data and duplicate it for the second sensor data, then shift the number of samples to represent 90 degrees of rotation. This is referred to as the "shifted-data" method. This approach is computationally efficient but has two drawbacks. The first is that the fidelity of the shift is limited to discrete samples. Thus, the angular precision is unlikely to produce a perfect 90-degree shift because the sample rate multiplied by 1/4 may not equate to 90 degrees of samples. This error is somewhat minimized by higher sample rates. The second deficiency is for cases in which the rotational speed is changing. The shifted number of samples will change periodically, and the result is a significant change to the resulting orbit plot.

The second method of simulating the second sensor channel is to use the derivative of the primary channel data. This approach works well for signals that are not overly sampled at a high rate because the differential will not be as noticeable. The prominent advantage is speed variations in the test article cause minimal effect, to the differential. While the derivative utilizes negligible processing power, and the difference calculation where the delta amount between each sample is calculated can be a suitable substitute. MATLAB has such a function called "diff", used for synthesizing the second channel of data, and it is referred to as the "derivative-diff" method.

The basis of this approach is best illustrated in Figure 1, wherein two sensors are located 90 degrees apart along the rotational axis of a rotating body, where ? defines the angle and direction of rotation. If the body is rigid and simple, then the signal picked up by the two sensors will be separated by 90 degrees and will each be a sinusoid. One sensor can be approximated by the sine of the angle of rotation and the other by the cosine of the angle, wherein the cosine is also the first derivative of the sine. Therefore, as shown the figure below, the sensor at 12 o'clock can be approximated by taking the derivative of the sensor at the 3 o'clock, and for a sampled system, shifting it by the number of samples associated with a 1/4 rotation of the body.

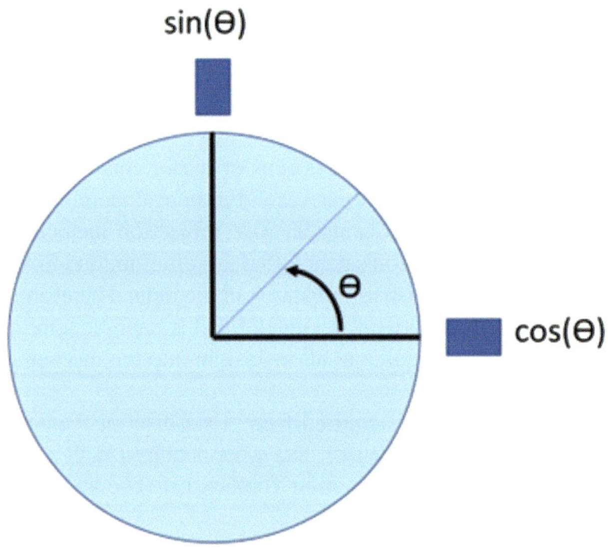

Fig. 1 Relationship of sensor position of a rotating body. Recall that the cosine is the derivative of the sine, which is also a 1/4 of the samples for one revolution.

Mechanical Fault Simulator

Figure 2 shows a mechanical fault simulator (MFS), including two main components: the driver and shaft assembly. A 250W (1/3 hp) induction motor drives the shaft from 0–66.5 Hz (0–4,000 rpm) via a lightweight aluminum precision flexible shaft coupling. The AISI 1060 shaft is supported by grease-lubricated clamp-on collar ball bearings with a nominal support distance of 0.7 m (28.5 in) and a shaft diameter of 12.7 mm (0.5 in.). Six 6061 aluminum balance discs are secured to the shaft, each with two keyless bushings. Each disc includes two balancing planes with 70 equally spaced bolt holes along the face of the disc for installing balancing weights. Eddy current proximity probes are in the horizontal and vertical orientations measuring the displacement at each disc. The acquisition system collected data at a sample rate of 16,384 samples/s.

The intent of this test rig was to create distinctly different sensor signatures and evaluate the performance of the deep learning algorithm. Therefore, data were collected at different mode shapes of the machine. When a rotating machine passes

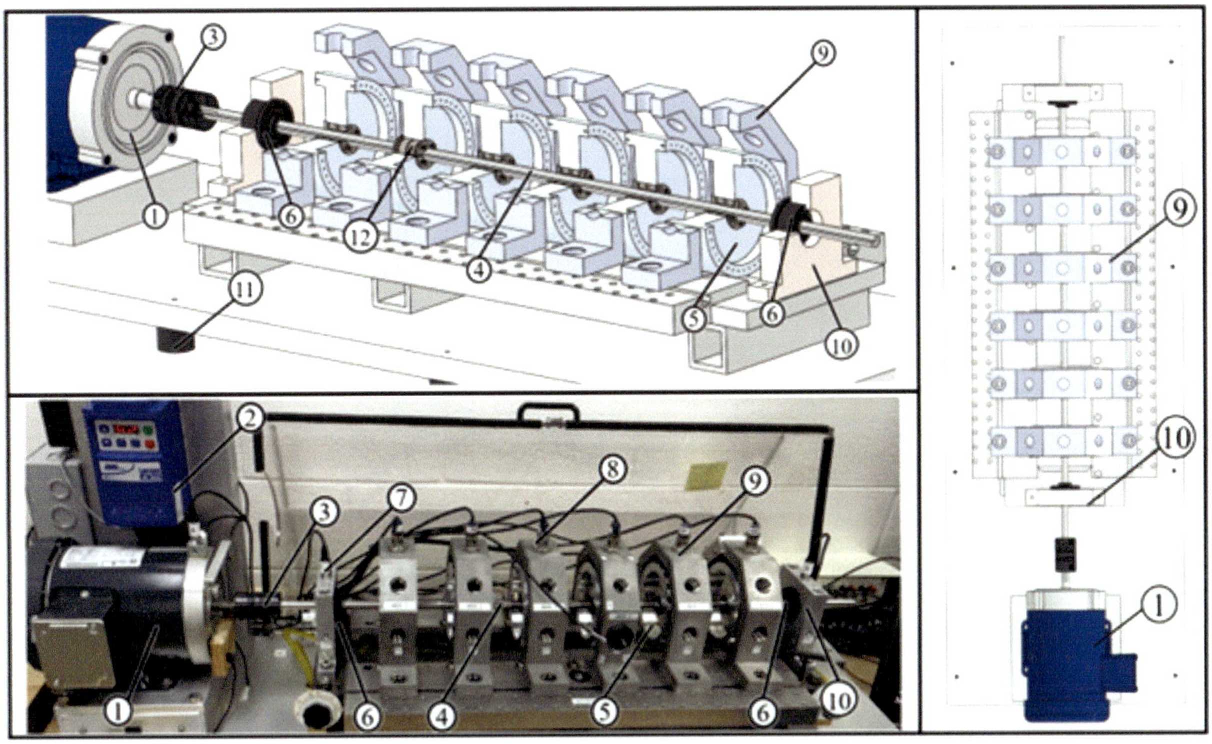

Fig. 2 Mechanical fault simulator (MFS): (1) motor, (2) VFD, (3) coupling, (4) shaft, (5) balancing wheel –qty 6, (6) ball bearing, (7) accelerometer, (8) proximity probe, (9) proximity probe mount (10) bearing pedestal, (11) rubber support, (12) keyless bushing.

through a natural frequency, the rotor operates in a different mode (i.e., the motion along the shaft is different) and thus a different signature will be obtained. For this test rig, the first natural frequency is a cylindrical (i.e., bounce) mode, the second natural frequency is a conical mode, and the third natural frequency is the first bending mode. (See Figure 1. 3 in ref [3], for a visual of the physical mode shapes.)

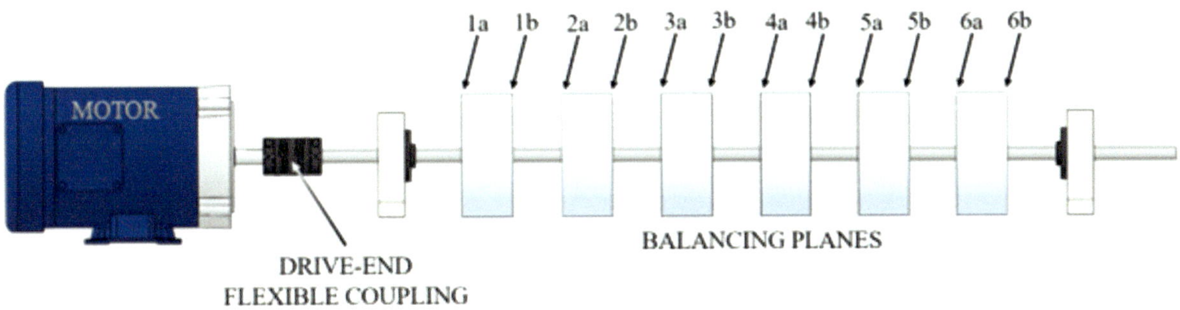

Fig. 3 Cross-sectional view of the rotor assembly, including the balancing planes (1a–6b), coupler, and driver. Each balancing wheel has two balancing planes spaced by approximately 2 in. where 2-56 size bolts were installed to balance the machine.

Additionally, each response signature was affected by the balancing discs, which had the three following configurations: (a) no alterations, (b) a single strip of aluminum tape, simulating a jump in amplitude once per revolution, and (c) 24 engraved lines simulating a drop in signal 24 times per revolution (Figure 4). The MFS provides 16 channels of data, including a tachometer, three accelerometers, and 12 proximity sensors. Three of the proximity sensors were tested at three different speeds, including 523 RPM (8.7 Hz), 1,300 RPM (21.6 Hz), and 4,386 RPM (73.1 Hz). The response described above for each type of balance wheel is shown in Table 1 below.

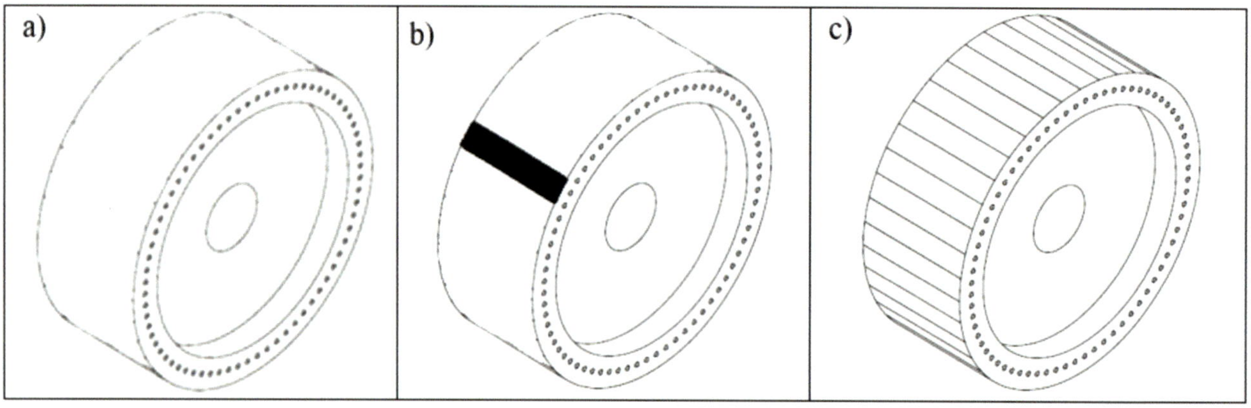

Fig. 4 Each balancing disc was black anodized in three patterns including blocking the signal of the proxy probe: (a) no distortion: third disc; (b) single piece of aluminum tape: fourth disc; (c) 40 inscribed lines: first and sixth disc.

Table 1 Orbit plots for the three different balance disc configurations at each natural frequency.

Natural frequency	No Distortion	Single strip	40 engraved lines
1st	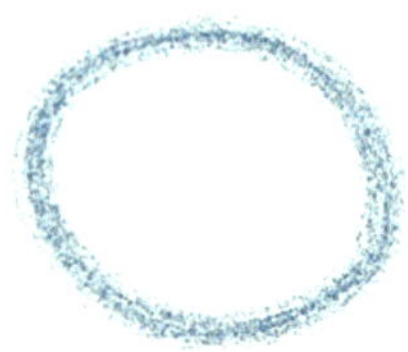		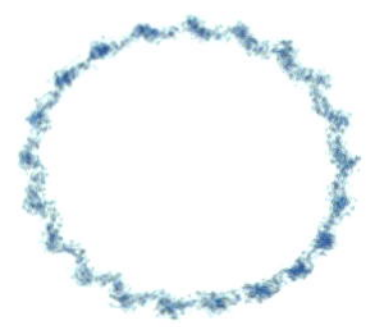
2nd	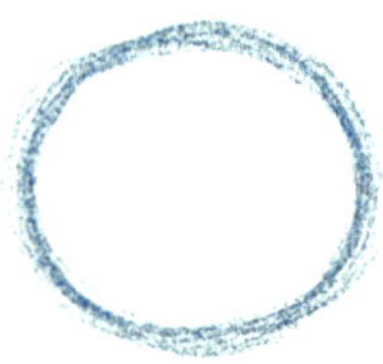	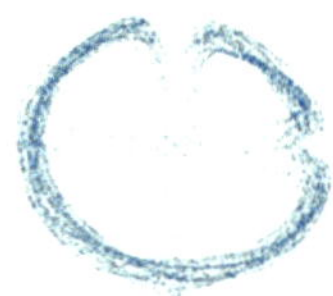	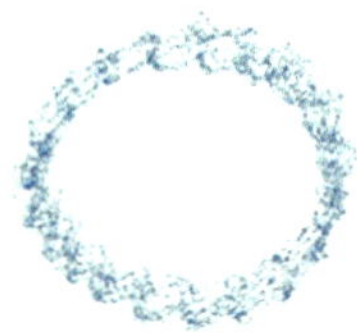
3rd		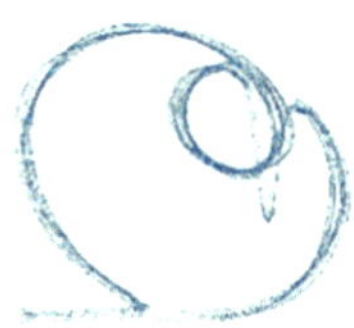	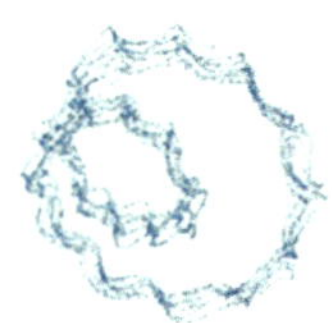

Data Preparation Process

Orbit plots were made using 10,000 data points, an image 368 x 598 px, and a plot character size of 15. These plots were reduced to 100 x 100 px PNG files, in gray scale with no axes annotation. One hundred deep learning iterations were used to obtain a comprehensive evaluation of the network training, and each deep learning session used a randomly chosen set of orbit plots for training. Of these orbit plots a few were set aside for testing the neural network. Each iteration was scored for training and testing accuracy. The stochastic gradient descent with momentum (SGDM) algorithm was used in all test cases for the simple convolutional neural network.

Simulated Data

The testing accuracy is defined as the ability of the trained network to recognize data from the same source as training/validation data. Simply put, this is similar to a face identifier but instead of a face, it identifies a simple 1D data sequence from a rotating machine. The unique features of the machine and its characteristics can be used as identification, similar to a fingerprint.

During early testing, it was observed that the training and testing of the neural network did not score above a 95% accuracy rate. It is theorized that systematic common mode data features from the MFS were contained in all the measurements and the training process could not fully differentiate between the channels. Therefore, a signal simulator was developed to produce a secondary set of data specifically for the deep learning process combining a weighted sum of a sinusoid signal and its first three harmonics, random noise, and a glitch generator. The amplitudes of all component signals were randomly set, within constraints, such that the resulting signals were all unique and produced a total of 100 signal combinations and 160 orbit plots for each signal combination.

Results

Three cases were compared to test the accuracy of the neural network to identify the data source. Both methods of 2D mapping were used which included the following cases: (1) using all sixteen channels from the MFS for all three speed conditions, (2) using only the higher-speed case for the MFS and omitting two of the accelerometers and one proximity sensor that provided marginal measurements, and (3) using 100 test cases from the signal simulator. Figure 5 reports the final accuracy results for the three test cases and includes the shifted-data and derivative-diff data mapping methods. The three test cases are the MFS data, MFS reduced data, and simulated data shown in Figure 5.

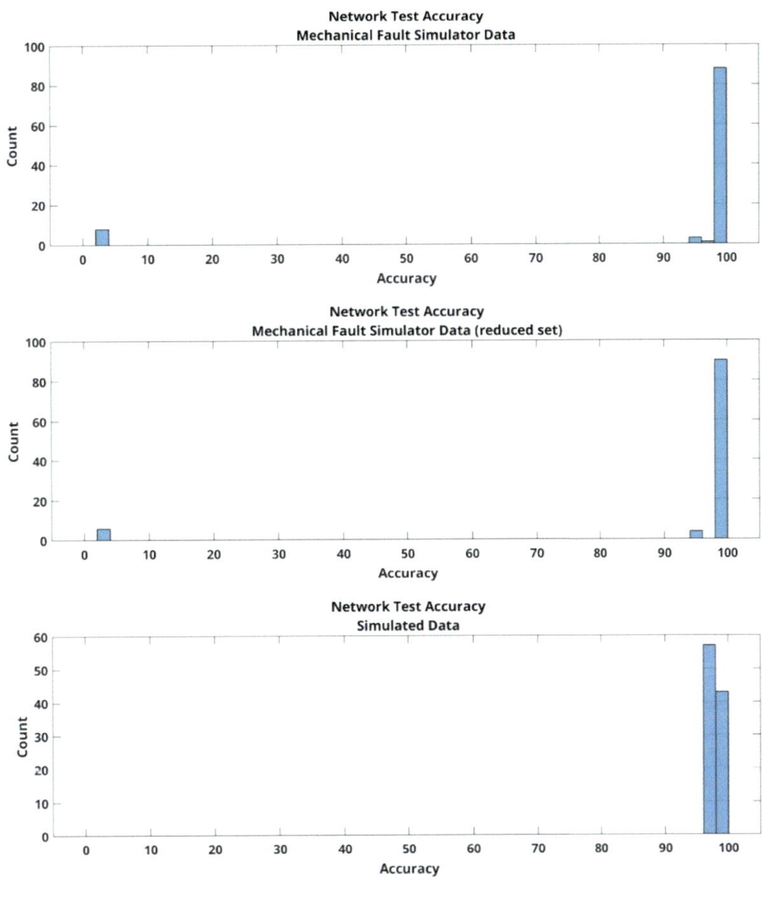

Fig. 5 Trained network accuracy for three test cases.

For the three cases, the plots show that the deep learning model performed accurately with the separately stored test data that was set aside. There are systematic features common to all the sensor channels so the real data performance could have been improved if it had originated from separate machines. Recall that the MFS data is all from the same rotating device. The simulated data on the other hand is independent of a physical device, hence lacks shared common characteristics associated with a physical device In all situations where the testing data shared common characteristics, the training accuracy reported by the deep learning model was poor. The training accuracy can serve as guidance for when not to use a neural network solution. For completeness, the poorer scoring accuracies are included herein but would most likely not be included in a real-world implementation.

The reduced set excludes the proximity probe channels that were malfunctioning. The simulated data was created by a signal generator model, with random noise and glitch features that were applied in such a way as to make the resulting data unique. The relationship in time and magnitude for the signals, noise and glitch characteristics were all randomly set. Because the simulated data was more unique and did not contain common features, it scored with a better accuracy

When testing the neural network against data it has never seen before, the results had high accuracy, mostly above 90%. For the first plot, there were data with an accuracy below 10%. What this means is that most of the proximity sensor data was accurately identified by the network by 90%, but there were around 3 bad channels that scored very poorly (like 10% accuracy success). For the reduced set, the middle plot, the data from the faulty proximity sensors were removed, which improved the middle plot with an accuracy of 95+% for all channels. Then for the last case with the simulated data, the results obtained were similar to the reduced set. All the simulated cases were accurately identified 96+% of the time.

Conclusion

By using a simple 2D mapping scheme for single-channel cyclic data, convolutional neural network trained with SGDM was able to train yield good data recognition results. The testing accuracy was typically above 94% for data produced from multiple sensors on the same rotating machine. The testing accuracy distribution changed but remained similar when several poorly performing channels were removed. For simulated data, the testing accuracy was above 96% for all test cases and conditions, including displacement measurements from the test rig. The neural network could accurately predict the source of data from a given set of sources at an accuracy of 94% or more. It is believed that the data from the MFS had common mode characteristics, or features, on all channels, thereby making it difficult for the deep learning algorithm to fully differentiate between each channel.

Opportunities for practical applications for this approach include machine diagnostics and performance optimization of rotating machines and engines. Two examples of using this method to diagnose machinery include fault conditions and engine tuning. Fault conditions could be characterized for a class of machines and then neural networks could be trained on the data. The resulting trained and validated neural network could then process and compare newly acquired data from other machines to determine if the systematic characteristics match. For engine tuning, data from an optimally tuned engine could be used to train a neural network to then analyze data acquired on other engines and determine whether optimal tuning was achieved.

References

1. Zhu, X., Hou, D., Zhou, P., Han, Z., Yuan, Y., Zhou, W., Yin, Q., "Rotor Fault Diagnosis Using a Convolutional Neural Network with Symmetrized Dot Pattern Images", vol 138, *Measurement*, 526–535, May 2019
2. *Get Started with Image Classification*. mathworks.com. https://www.mathworks.com/help/deeplearning/gs/create-simple-image-classification-network-using-deep-network-designer.html (accessed October 3, 2024)
3. Glick, Z. C., "The Axisymmetric Harmonic Element Including Gyroscopic Effects: A Complete Derivation", *Rose-Hulman Institute of Technology*, August 2019
4. Jeong, H., Park, S., Woo, S., and Lee, S., "Rotating Machinery Diagnostics using Deep Learning on Orbit Plot Images", *Procedia Manufacturing Rotating Machinery Diagnostics using Deep Learning on Orbit Plot Images*, vol 5, 1107–1118, 2016
5. Caponetto, R., Rizzo, F., Russotti, L., and Xibilia, M. G., "Deep Learning Algorithm for Predictive Maintenance of Rotating Machines Through the Analysis of the Orbits Shape of the Rotor Shaft", *Proceedings of the 1st International Conference on Smart Innovation, Ergonomics and Applied Human Factors (SEAHF). SEAHF 2019. Smart Innovation, Systems and Technologies*, vol 150, 245–250, June 2019

This manuscript has been authored by UT-Battelle, LLC under Contract No. DE-AC05-00OR22725 with the U.S. Department of Energy.

Chapter 3
Towards PEAR: a Benchmark Dataset for Population-based SHM

Connor O'Higgins, David Hester, Keith Worden, and Daniel S. Brennan

Abstract Population-based Structural Health Monitoring (PBSHM) is a developing approach in Structural Health Monitoring (SHM) that leverages data from multiple structure's to enhance the understanding of an individual structures health. Where traditional SHM utilises only a single structure's data, PBSHM utilises the collective knowledge from a population of structures. A pivotal component for facilitating the aforementioned collective knowledge is transfer learning: the ability to infer knowledge from a source structure to a target structure within the population. To ensure the transferred knowledge enhances rather than hinders the target structure, a degree of structural similarity is first established.

Both sub procedures of PBSHM require robust data modelling, which in turn requires substantial amounts of high-quality data; something that with PBSHM in its infancy is not openly available for researchers to benchmark algorithms against. In this study, the aim is to address this data shortfall of PBSHM by developing a comprehensive dataset of semi-realistic bridge models. This dataset is intended to serve as a test bed for developing, benchmarking, and validating PBSHM algorithms, particularly focussing in on the necessitated data for similarity metrics and transfer-learning techniques. Subsequently, it is explored how the proposed dataset can be expanded to include additional structures and discuss the potential applications of the dataset in advancing PBSHM research.

Keywords Population-based structural health monitoring · Benchmark dataset · Irreducible element model · Bridges · Machine learning

Introduction

In structural health monitoring (SHM), the availability of benchmark datasets, like the S101 [1] and Z24 [2] bridge datasets, have been instrumental in advancing the field. These datasets provide researchers with a common platform to test, validate, and compare the performance of new SHM methods and algorithms. However, in the emerging field of PBSHM, no such benchmark datasets currently exist. This is partly because of the relatively recent development of PBSHM, but also in part because any PBSHM benchmark dataset would inherently require data from multiple structures to form a population, thus gathering such a dataset is inevitably more complex.

As a potential solution to this problem, this paper proposes the curation of PBSHM dataset consisting of synthetic structures based on real-world engineering principles: Population-based SHM Engineered Asset Resource (PEAR). The aforementioned PEAR dataset will serve as the benchmark for future research to be evaluated against within the PBSHM community. The breadth of knowledge required to generate synthetic structures across the range of PBSHM structure is vast; therefore, the goal of this paper is not to create an immutable dataset, rather establish the fundamentals required to facilitate an evolutionary approach to including new structures and associated data within the dataset. To provide an initial set of structures, this paper uses beam-and-slab bridges.

Connor O'Higgins · David Hester
School of Natural and Built Environment, Queen's University of Belfast, Stranmillis Road, Belfast, BT9 5AG, UK
e-mail: c.ohggins@qub.ac.uk; d.hester@qub.ac.uk

Keith Worden · Daniel S. Brennan
Dynamics Research Group, School of Mechanical, Aerospace, and Civil Engineering, University of Sheffield, Mappin Street, Sheffield, S1 3TD, UK
e-mail: k.worden@sheffield.ac.uk; d.s.brennan@sheffield.ac.uk

Thomas Matarazzo et al. (eds.), *Data Science in Engineering, Vol. 11*, Conference Proceedings of the Society for Experimental Mechanics Series, https://doi.org/10.13052/9788743801566-3

This paper follows the following flow: firstly an overview of PBSHM is given with details on existing databases, schemas, and benchmark datasets, thus motivating this work. The next section outlines the design process for both the overall dataset and the individual sub-datasets contained within, detailing the key requirements for ensuring that the dataset can become an effective benchmarking tool for the community. After the description of the dataset, a detailed example of the first stage in developing a sub-dataset is presented, including the procedures used to design realistic structures for the sub-dataset and the outputs required for inclusion in a PBSHM database. Finally, the conclusions are presented to explore considerations regarding the current dataset, its future expansion, and the potential paths for further development to enhance its utility in PBSHM research.

Background

Population-Based Structural Health Monitoring (PBSHM) focusses on the analysis of data from multiple structures within a related population, providing valuable insights into both the population as a whole and individual structures within it [3]. Unlike traditional Structural Health Monitoring (SHM) methods that concentrate on a single structure, PBSHM allows for the application of methods such as transfer learning. Transfer learning involves applying knowledge gained from one task to improve performance on a different but related task. Instead of starting from scratch with each new task, models trained on one structure can be adapted for use on others, leveraging shared knowledge to enhance the accuracy of a given model. However, for transfer learning to be effective in the context of PBSHM, it is crucial to ensure that structural similarities are well understood to avoid negative transfer. To address this, Irreducible Element (IE) models, combined with graph-based approaches, play a key role in identifying structural similarities and variations.

This framework of finding similarities between the structures to inform where transfer learning is appropriate mitigates the risks of negative transfer. Further foundational details on PBSHM can be found in works such as [4, 5, 6, 7]. One of the main challenges in the emerging field of PBSHM is the scarcity of data for similar populations of structures. This has been addressed in several studies where [8] collected data from four beam-and-slab bridges and two pedestrian footbridges. [9] and [10] simulated a population of 10 degrees of freedom and toy structures to validate a PBSHM transfer-learning method and a graph-matching algorithm, respectively. It is believed that PBSHM benchmark datasets would aid in the development of PBSHM research. These datasets will play a part in developing and validating PBSHM methods.

PEAR Foundations

The premise behind the Population-based SHM Engineered Asset Resource (PEAR) dataset, is to provide a set of known reference data to enable PBSHM algorithms to be developed, evaluated, and validated against. As alluded to in the previous sections of this paper, building a dataset to cover the full remit of potential PBSHM algorithms and applications is no trivial task; therefore, this goal will need to be achieved over time via multiple expansions and iterations to PEAR. As such it would be naive to believe that all of these expansions and iterations to PEAR will be done by the authors of this paper; consequently, the first portion of this paper will be focussed on setting a list of requirements, structures, and stages necessitated to enable growth of PEAR by the PBSHM community.

PEAR foundations: requirements

The purpose of the requirement's section of the PEAR Foundations is to provide a guide for the type of data that should be included within PEAR.

Requirement 1: A key requirement for the dataset is that it should be suitable as a testbed for both current and emerging PBSHM methods and techniques. This includes facilitating the development and evaluation of approaches such as transfer learning, which allows for the application of knowledge from one structure to another within a population. The dataset should support the comparison of structures via similarity metrics such as IE models and graph-matching algorithms, as this is a vital step in the transfer of knowledge between structures. The dataset should also be well-suited for the application of various machine learning methods, providing a source of data for training and validating machine-learning models.

Requirement 2: The dataset should be searchable, allowing users to find and extract subsets of the data easily. This functionality is aimed at making the database more user-friendly, enabling researchers to focus on specific types of structures or specific structure configurations relevant to their studies. To meet this requirement, the dataset must be properly indexed, ensuring that all relevant variables, such as structure type or number of spans (for bridge structures), can be queried and filtered from the database.

Requirement 3: The methods used to design the structures in the dataset should be clear, transparent, and, where possible, rooted in real-world structural design practices; this ensures that the generated structures are representative of real-world structures. Additionally, the variations in the structures, such as span lengths for brides, beam sizes, and deck thicknesses, should reflect the diversity found in actual structures, or in the case of the dataset described in this paper, in real-world bridge stocks.

Requirement 4: Since the inception of PBSHM, it has been understood that providing a shared-data domain for which PBSHM data resides, is crucial in seeing wide-scale adoption of the technology. The recently-published work by Brennan et al. [7] introduce the PBSHM schema as the domain in which the PBSHM data gets regulated into the same standardised data form. As such, the dataset will store its data in the PBSHM schema format and any additions to the dataset will have to adhere to this. If there is not an area within the PBSHM schema to store the relevant data, a new extension to the PBSHM Schema must be proposed and included within the next update.

PEAR foundations: structure

Designing the dataset's structure is important to ensure effective data retrieval and utilisation. A well-structured dataset will facilitate users to quickly access the specific data they need, making it easier to perform tasks with the datasets and subsets of the data. The purpose of the structure section within the PEAR Foundations, is to not only organise the dataset's data into a logical order for easy retrieval of data, but to also facilitate the required expansion of new data within the dataset, without invalidating any existing dataset data. Figure 1 depicts the four hierarchical categorisations of data within PEAR: root category, subtype, parameter set, and scenario. To best explain how these categories interact with each other, the example of a file system will be used.

Root Category
↓
Subtype
↓
Parameter Set
↓
Scenario

Fig. 1 The hierarchical structure of the PEAR dataset.

At the root of the filesystem, there will be a 'PEAR' folder. Within the 'PEAR' folder there will be a folder for every 'root category'. Inside each 'root category' folder there will be a folder for every 'subtype'. Inside the 'subtype' folders will be a folder for every 'parameter set'. Inside a 'parameter set' folder their will be the first occurance of PBSHM data within the filesystem. The 'parameter set' folder will include a description file which outlines the allowable variations within the hyperparameters for that 'parameter set'. Additionally, Stage 0 and Stage 1 data files — see the following sections for details — will also be stored within this folder. Within the 'parameter set' folder there will also be folders for each 'scenario'. Inside the 'scenario' folder will be Stage 2+ data files — again see the following section for details.

A 'root category' would be any category of structure which would normally not be categorised with another, for instance two root categories could be aeroplane and bridge. A 'subtype' would be a categorisation within a 'root category' to differentiate purpose or style, for instance within the aeroplane 'root category' one could have two 'subtypes' of narrow-body and wide-body. Conversely, within the bridge 'root category' one could have 'subtypes' of truss and suspension. The 'parameter set' is a named group of hyperparameters within the subtype to generate the Stage 0 and Stage 1 data files. These hyperparameters are specific to the 'subtype' and enable different values of the 'subtype' hyperparameters to generate unique Stage 0 and Stage 1 data. The 'scenario' is a named group of action(s) performed on the Stage 1 data of the 'parameter set' to generate Stage 2+ PBSHM data.

During the initial planning for PEAR, three initial 'root categories' of structures were identified for inclusion within the dataset: bridges, masts, and wind turbines. Figure 2 shows the initial dataset hierarchy using the PEAR Foundations structure.

PEAR
- 1. Bridges
  - 1.1 Beam and slab
  - 1.2 Ladder deck
  - 1.3 Truss
- 2. Wind turbines
  - 2.1 Monopole
- 3. Masts
  - 3.1 Lattice tower
  - 3.2 High guided
  - 3.3 Monopole

Fig. 2 The initial 'root categories' and 'subtypes' for PEAR

PEAR foundations: stages

As discussed, PEAR has been designed from the ground up to mutate over time via iterations and expansion of the data included within. The purpose of the stage's section within the PEAR Foundations is to provide known 'save points' within the dataset to facilitate collaboration across the multidisciplinary areas of knowledge within PBSHM. The PEAR dataset by necessity, must contain data for both the 'similarities' portion of PBSHM, but also the knowledge transfer portion of PBSHM; therefore, it must be a supported workflow to have one team design and build the IE models (Stage 1 data) within the dataset, and another team to then build the simulations to generate Stage 2+ data. To support this distributed workflow, each stage must therefore only rely upon data being available from the previous stage, for instance a Stage 2 data process, must only rely upon the data being present for Stages 0 and Stage 1.

For a sub-dataset to be included in PEAR, the minimum requirement is the 'parameter set' description file, and a completion of Stage 0 & 1. Once a dataset is produced, it is given a reference within PEAR. Once this reference has been produced, the individual structures within that sub-dataset will remain unchanged to ensure consistency and reproducibility of results. The specific subcategories for Stage 2+ are not rigidly defined, providing researchers the freedom to choose the most appropriate structural responses for their research.

The stages described below are designed to be generic and applicable to all sub-datasets regardless of the 'root category' and 'subtype'.

Stage 0: Structure Design. In this initial stage, realistic structures are designed with pseudo-random properties from the range of hyperparameters set within the 'parameter set'. A Structural Information (SI) model and structural report are produced for each generated structure. The report provides a detailed description of the structure in a human-interpretable way, and the SI model provides a computer-interpretable way for indexing and querying each structure included within the dataset. A 'parameter set' with only Stage 0 models is not a valid 'save point'; a Stage 0 model must always be accompanied by an associated Stage 1 model to be a valid 'save point'.

Stage 1: IE Models. In this stage, IE models are generated for each SI model present within the 'parameter set'. Depending upon the hyperparameters set within the 'parameter set', this may include generating detailed IE models, Canonical Form IE models, or any future IE model type yet to be declared. This is the first stage where a process may stop, and multiple independent processes continue to generate Stage 2+ data.

Stage 2+ Scenario Data. Using the data from Stage 0 and Stage 1, a simulated scenario can then be run on the generated IE models. How this scenario is simulated is outside the purview of the PEAR Foundations; however, the response from the simulation must be saved back into the PEAR dataset as a valid PBSHM Schema document. Possible, but not limited to scenarios are: static load displacements, natural frequencies, mode shapes, and frequency response functions. A scenario is not limited to treating the structure from the associated IE model as a 'healthy' structure, a scenario may introduce 'damage' into the model before performing its simulation and saving the response back into a PBSHM Schema document.

Populating PEAR

In this section of the paper, we look at how to populate PEAR with its first initial sub-dataset to the minimum stages defined above: a beam and slab bridge sub-dataset to Stage 1. For this example, the 'root category' is stated to be 'bridges' with a 'subtype' within that 'root category' of 'beam-and-slab'. This will first start by providing a definition and description of their general form. The procedures used to design a semi-realistic beam and slab bridge model for our sub-dataset will then be presented, ensuring these models are representative of real-world structures. Where appropriate, the decisions made during the design process will be explained with reference to established principles from bridge engineering. This will help clarify how the models are rooted in practical engineering knowledge and the balance one has taken between realism and the constraints imposed by the simulation of thousands of structures.

Beam-and-slab bridges were selected for the initial sub-dataset test structure because of their prevalence, particularly within the UK. Beam-and-slab bridges are one of the most common forms of concrete highway bridge construction as they offer a straightforward and economic bridge solution, with readily-available standard sections and a relatively high speed of construction. Their simplicity in design and construction makes them ideal candidates for this study, especially since their widespread use means there are well-established design rules to guide the design of these structures. These design rules allow one to create realistic structures that are grounded in practical engineering while ensuring consistency and reliability across the dataset.

Populating PEAR: general from

The general form of a beam-and-slab bridge consists of precast concrete beams that serve as the primary structural components of the bridge. These beams are typically lifted into place, where they are supported by piers or abutments that have been constructed in advance. Once the beams are positioned, an *in situ* concrete deck is poured over them to form the main deck of the bridge.

Below are the main components and a brief description of a typical beam and slab bridge:

1. Precast Prestressed Bridge Beams: These are the primary load-bearing components of the bridge. Precast off-site and prestressed to increase their load-carrying capacity, these beams are designed to resist the main traffic loads of the bridge.
2. Reinforced Concrete Deck: The reinforced concrete deck is poured in situ on top of the precast beams, forming the main surface of the bridge. Reinforcement bars are embedded within the concrete for strength.
3. Diaphragm: The diaphragm is a transverse structural element placed between the bridge beams. Its primary function is to distribute loads evenly across the bridge and provide lateral stability, and help transfer load to the supporting structure of the bridge.
4. Columns: Columns are vertical structural supports that transfer the load from the bridge deck and beams down to the foundation.

Populating PEAR: variables

This section will outline the structural variations that will be modelled within the beam and slab bridge sub-dataset, and will describe the key variables that will be adjusted from one bridge model to another, such as beam dimensions, span lengths, and deck thickness. The procedure employed to ensure that these variations result in semi-realistic bridge models will also be outlined. By randomly varying these parameters, the aim is to reflect a range of real-world scenarios while maintaining a level of consistency and realism that supports the effective evaluation of PBSHM methodologies. This approach will help ensure that the dataset provides a robust testbed for examining the performance of transfer learning techniques and other PBSHM methods across diverse bridge configurations. The variables are categorised into two main groups:

- General Bridge Variables: These include aspects that affect the overall bridge configuration and performance, such as number of spans, width of bridge and material properties. The procedures for selecting these variables ensure that each bridge model reflects realistic scenarios that may be found in the real world.
- Element Geometry Variables: This category covers the specific dimensions and geometrical features of individual bridge elements, such as beam dimensions and diaphragm heights. The procedures for these variables involve selecting specific element geometries that would be suitable so that the bridge can support the typical traffic loads that would be encountered.

Some variables are selected randomly from a predefined list, such as the number of spans and deck thickness. Other variables are dependent on prior selections, for instance, the diaphragm height, which is set to match the height of the primary beam. Additionally, certain variables, such as the geometric properties of the bridge beams, are selected from appropriate manufacturer technical documents. For this work, the Shay Murtagh Technical Manual [11] was used, although any equivalent design guide could be substituted. A detailed description of each variable and the procedure used to select them can be found in Table 1, located in Appendix A.

Populating PEAR: outputs

For each bridge, a short report will detail all the key properties, including both General Bridge Variables and Element Geometry Variables. This report will also include drawings of the bridge structure. The individual structure reports are designed to provide users of the dataset with a quick overview of each beam and slab bridge structure. These reports contain the bridge details for each structure in a standard table. An example of the table included in each of the reports is given below. Each report also includes a set of standardised bridge drawings that show the general arrangement of the main structural elements for each bridge. The drawings include:

- Cross-Section Through the Deck: shows the arrangement of the main bridge beams and deck slab
- Cross-Section Through the Support: shows the arrangement of the bridge beams, diaphragms, and columns if included in the structure.
- Elevation of the Bridge: The elevation provides a side view of the bridge, showing the overall span arrangement.
- Plan of the Bridge Showing the Superstructure: This top-down view showing the arrangement of the bridge beams and diaphragms.

Individual Structure Reports

The individual structure reports are designed to provide users of the dataset with a quick overview of each beam-and-slab bridge structure. These reports contain the bridge details for each structure in a standard table. An example of the table included in each of the reports is included within the appendices.

Each report also includes a set of standardised bridge drawings that show the general arrangement of the main structural elements for each bridge. Figure 3 shows an example of the bridge drawings included in the reports.

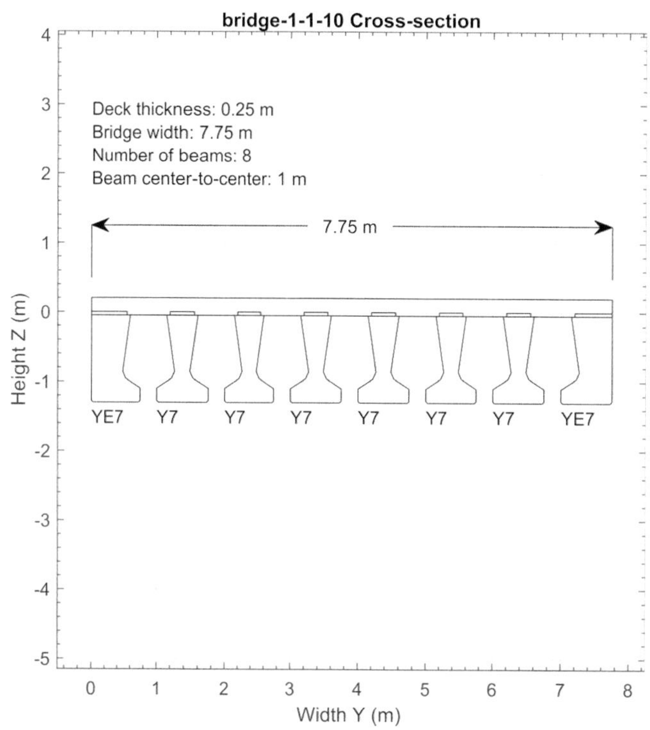

Fig. 3 Example of bridge drawings, cross-section through deck

Structural Information Models

Each bridge will be accompanied by a Structural Information (SI) model that contains all the bridge's properties in a format compatible with the dataset's database (JSON format), allowing for efficient data retrieval about the individual structures. The SI models contain all the necessary data to describe each beam-and-slab bridge structure fully. These models are stored in JSON format, to allow easy integration into the broader PBSHM Framework. The use of JSON ensures that the information models can be efficiently stored and queried by the framework. Each Structural Information model contains a comprehensive set of data points, covering both general bridge variables and element geometry variables; this includes details such as span lengths, beam dimensions, deck thickness, and material properties. The structured nature of these models allows users to obtain all relevant information about a bridge in a single, easily interpretable file. Beyond serving as a detailed record for each structure, the SI models will be used for database integration. Users can leverage the information models to filter and identify specific subsets of bridges based on defined criteria, such as finding all bridges with a certain number of spans or selecting bridges with specific material properties. This capability ensures that the dataset is flexible and can be adapted for various PBSHM research tasks.

Dataset Statistics

The dataset statistics are designed to provide an overview of the beam and slab bridge structures included in the dataset. These statistics offer insights into the distribution of key variables across the dataset, allowing users to better understand the variability of the generated structures. The primary focus of the statistics is on the distributions of the bridge variables, such as the number of spans, beam dimensions, deck thickness, and material properties. For instance, one important statistic is the distribution of the number of spans in the dataset, which provides information on the range of bridge configurations included in the dataset. In addition to providing an overview, the dataset statistics also aid in validating the design process. For variables that are randomly selected from a defined set of values, the statistics can help confirm that the variable has the expected distribution. For example, if a variable such as span length is randomly chosen from a predefined set of values, the resulting distribution in the dataset should be roughly even; this ensures that no unintended biases have been introduced during the generation of the bridge models. Other variables that are dependent on other factors are expected to have different distributions. Figure 4 gives an example of the distribution of number of spans and number of primary beams from a dataset that contains one thousand structures.

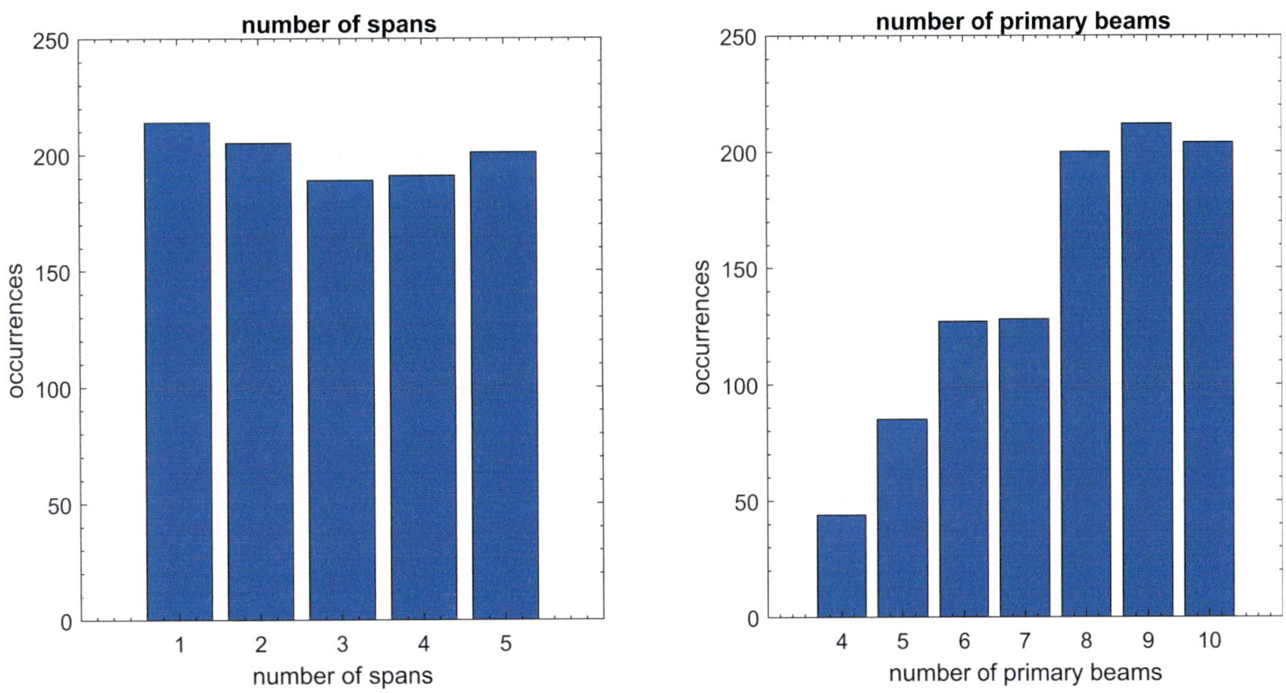

Fig. 4 Example of dataset statistics, number of spans and number of primary beams

Conclusion

In this work, the foundations have been laid for the PEAR benchmark PBSHM dataset by defining its core requirements, structure, and stages. By establishing a structured approach to creating sub-datasets, starting with beam-and-slab bridges presented in this work, the aim is to ensure consistency in the structures and structures that are grounded in sound engineering design practice.

For the future development of this work, the next step involves extending the process outlined in this paper to other types of bridges, such as ladder-deck and truss bridges, as well as to masts and wind turbine structures. Once the initial PEAR dataset is populated, researchers will have the opportunity to suggest or develop additional types of structures or perform new structural simulations on existing datasets, with the aim of enhancing the datasets for their particular research needs.

The potential use of PEAR in the development of PBSHM methods is widespread. It can be used to train and validate machine-learning algorithms, develop transfer-learning methods, and evaluate their performance across different structure types. Although developed with PBSHM as a focus, PEAR should be equally suited for the development and validation of traditional SHM methods; this potential may be investigated in a future piece of work.

Via continued expansion and refinement of the work presented here, it is hoped that PEAR will serve as a valuable tool for advancing PBSHM research.

Acknowledgments The authors of this paper gratefully acknowledge the support of the UK Engineering and Physical Sciences Research Council (EPSRC) via grant reference EP/W005816/1. For the purpose of open access, the authors have applied a Creative Commons Attribution (CC BY) licence to any Author Accepted Manuscript version arising.

References

1. Michael Döhler, Falk Hille, Laurent Mevel, and Werner Rücker. "Structural health monitoring with statistical methods during progressive damage test of s101 bridge". *Engineering Structures*, 69:183–193, 6 2014.
2. Bart Peeters and Guido De Roeck. "One-year monitoring of the z24-bridge: environmental effects versus damage events". 30:149–171, 2 2001.
3. Keith Worden, Lawrence A. Bull, Paul Gardner, Julian Gosliga, Timothy J. Rogers, Elizabeth J. Cross, Evangelos Papatheou, Weijiang Lin, and Nikolaos Dervilis. "A brief introduction to recent developments in population-based structural health monitoring". *Frontiers in Built Environment*, 6, 9 2020.
4. J. Gosliga, P.A. Gardner, L.A. Bull, N. Dervilis, and K. Worden. "Foundations of Population-based SHM, Part II: Heterogeneous populations – Graphs, networks, and communities". *Mechanical Systems and Signal Processing*, 148:107144, 2 2021.
5. P. Gardner, L.A. Bull, J. Gosliga, N. Dervilis, and K. Worden. "Foundations of population-based SHM, Part III: Heterogeneous populations – Mapping and transfer". *Mechanical Systems and Signal Processing*, 149:107142, 2 2021.
6. G. Tsialiamanis, C. Mylonas, E. Chatzi, N. Dervilis, D.J. Wagg, and K. Worden. "Foundations of population-based SHM, Part IV: The geometry of spaces of structures and their feature spaces". *Mechanical Systems and Signal Processing*, 157:107692, 8 2021.
7. Daniel S. Brennan, Julian Gosliga, Elizabeth J. Cross, and Keith Worden. "Foundations of population-based SHM, Part V: Network, framework and Database". *Mechanical Systems and Signal Processing*, 223:111602, 1 2025.
8. Andrew Bunce, Daniel S. Brennan, Alan Ferguson, Connor O'Higgins, Su Taylor, Elizabeth J Cross, Keith Worden, James Brownjohn, and David Hester. "On population-based structural health monitoring for bridges: Comparing similarity metrics and dynamic responses between sets of bridges". *Mechanical Systems and Signal Processing*, 216:111501, 7 2024.
9. A.J. Hughes, R.J. Barthorpe, N. Dervilis, C.R. Farrar, and K. Worden. "A probabilistic risk-based decision framework for structural health monitoring". *Mechanical Systems and Signal Processing*, 150:107339, 3 2021.
10. Daniel S Brennan, Timothy J Rogers, Elizabeth J Cross, and Keith Worden. "On calculating structural similarity metrics in population-based structural health monitoring". *Accepted in Data Centric Engineering*, 2024.
11. Shay Murtagh. "Technical manual, prestressed concrete beams". Technical report, 2014.

Appendices

Table 1 The available hyperparameters within the proposed 1.1 dataset.

Parameter	Description	Selection process
Number of spans	Total number of bridge spans	Spans for beam and slab bridges are typically between 1 and 5 spans, so the number of spans is randomly selected from this range.

Length of spans	Individual length of each span of the bridge	The maximum length of the span is dictated by the bridge beams and what they are rated for. The other consideration is that the length of span for a given bridge is typical of a similar length. E.g. you don't typically have a 5 m span and a 50 m span in the same bridge. The maximum variation of spans is set to be 70%
Number of primary beams	The number of primary bridge beams across the width of the bridge	This is dictated by the width of the deck and the recommended spacing of the bridge beams
Width of deck	The width of the bridge deck	The overall approximate size of the deck is randomly chosen between 6 m and 20 m. This range accommodated typical roads ranging from a single carriage to a 4-lane motorway with a hard shoulder lane. The final specific width of the road may be adjusted to fit into the recommended spacing of the bridge beams.
Thickness of deck	The thickness of the reinforced concrete deck	The thickness of the deck is randomly chosen from 0.15 m to 0.3 m as this would be the typical thickness of a deck in a beam and slab bridge.
Beam centre to centre	The centre to centre distance between the primary bridge beams	This is taken from the bridge beam technical manual.
Column ends	Binary variable: are there columns located at each end of the bridge	Randomly chosen to have or not have columns at the two ends of the bridge.
Column middle	Binary variable: are there columns located at the intermediary supports of the Bridge	Columns were randomly chosen to have or not have at the intermediate supports of the bridge. However, if the structure has columns at the ends and is greater than one span, then 'Column middle' is set to 1.
Column number	The number of columns (if present) per support of the bridge	The number of columns is chosen randomly (if present) from 2 (the minimum needed to provide support) to the number of primary beams. The columns are typically used to support the primary beams of the structure.
Column height	The height of the columns (if present)	The height of the columns is randomly chosen from 5 m to 8 m (0.5 increments). This height is the minimum required, as stated by UK government standards, and the maximum is chosen to be a sensible upper limit that a typical bridge would have.
Column diameter	The Diameter of the columns (if present)	Randomly chosen to be between 0.5 m and 1.0 m in 0.1 m increments.
Diaphragm height	The height of the diaphragm	This is the depth of the primary beam so that the diaphragm lies between the deck and the top of the columns.
Primary beam geometry	The bridge beam reference that defined the cross-sectional geometry of the primary Beams	The primary beam geometry is decided by starting with a list of all the most common bridge beam types, eliminating any that would not be suitable for the larger span length and bridge width and then randomly choosing from the remaining allowable bridge beams.
Edge beam geometry	The bridge beam reference that defined the cross-sectional geometry of the edge beams (if different from the primary beams)	Some of the bridge beams require different geometry for the two outer edge beams. If this is the case, each primary beam that needs a different edge beam will have a complementary edge beam, which is selected as required.
Diaphragm width	The width of the diaphragm	Random between 0.8 m and 1.6 m because this is the typical width of diaphragms.

Chapter 4
The Use of Machine Learning in Improved Hydrostatic Load Prediction for Inland Waterways Navigation Infrastructure

Mayank Chadha, Ying Zhao, Zhen Hu, and Michael D. Todd

Abstract The miter gate structure is a crucial infrastructure component that regulates waterway traffic and, therefore, can benefit from continuous health monitoring. Our past effort to build a decision-support digital twin of the miter gate structure requires creating a high-fidelity finite element model and its equivalent digital surrogate, capable of modeling the lifecycle of the structure. The primary loading that the miter gate is subjected to includes the upstream and downstream hydrostatic head. Therefore, the damage state of the miter gate depends on the operations of the gate (how many times the gate is opened and closed) as well as the river discharge. In our previous work, we assumed a statistical model to capture the water heads. However, better prognostics of the gate demand better knowledge of future river discharge. Traditional river routing methods are constrained by numerous assumptions and often result in noisy forecasts that diverge from true gauged values. We propose hybrid river discharge forecast models that integrate physics-based prediction models with state-of-the-art machine learning techniques. The proposed hybrid models leverage runoff data from the entire watershed, address the variability of the currently used traditional physics-based model predictions, and utilize advanced data-driven algorithms to forecast river discharge. This integration not only enhances the precision of discharge forecasts but also significantly improves the decision-support systems for miter gate structures and other real-world problems that require discharge forecasts.

Keywords Physics-Enhanced Machine Learning · Miter Gates · Hybrid Modeling · Lifecycle Management

Introduction

Our ongoing research efforts in lifecycle asset management focus on river-related assets, primarily dams and miter gates [1–2]. The goal is to build a comprehensive structural model that is capable of (a) simulating the lifecycle of the structure while considering uncertainties in loading; (b) being updated to reflect the current state of the structure, diagnosed using sensor data obtained through a Structural Health Monitoring (SHM) system (model updating); (c) forecasting the future state of the structure for an assumed loading time series and determining the remaining useful life (prognostics); and (d) guiding decision-making regarding the operations and maintenance of the structure.

In the case of river-based structures, such as dams and miter gates, the primary external load is the upstream and downstream water head, which is directly connected to the river's discharge. Therefore, a key aspect of understanding the future behavior of the structure, albeit probabilistically, is to utilize a reasonable model for the water heads, which, in turn, are connected to the river discharge. Consequently, it is valuable to develop a more accurate discharge predictive model that could feed into the comprehensive structural model and help engineers better understand how the structure might behave in the medium-term future (such as over a year).

In our parallel ongoing research efforts, we have developed better, more reliable, physics-guided, data-driven, and probabilistic river discharge forecast models [3,4]. In this article, we detail the effectiveness of the hybrid discharge forecasting model and outline potential applications in lifecycle asset modeling and decision-making.

Mayank Chadha · Michael D. Todd
Department of Structural Engineering, University of California San Diego, La Jolla, CA 92093, USA
e-mail: machadha@ucsd.edu; mdtodd@ucsd.edu

Ying Zhao · Zhen Hu
Department of Industrial and Manufacturing Systems Engineering, University of Michigan-Dearborn, Dearborn, MI 48128, USA
e-mail: yinzhao@umich.edu; zhennhu@umich.edu

Thomas Matarazzo et al. (eds.), *Data Science in Engineering, Vol. 11*, Conference Proceedings of the Society for Experimental Mechanics Series, https://doi.org/10.13052/9788743801566-4

Hybrid Modeling for River Discharge Forecasting

The National Water Information System (NWIS), operated by the U.S. Geological Survey (USGS), is the primary source of streamflow data in the United States. However, as of 2023, only 10,996 sites have automated monitoring systems to track current stream conditions. This is a small fraction considering the U.S. has around 250,000 rivers and over 3.5 million miles of waterways. The scarcity of discharge measurements from gauged locations makes stream and waterway predictions challenging. As a result, alternative methods, such as the Routing Application for Parallel Computation of Discharge (RAPID) model, are often used to estimate flows [5–8].

For this study, we considered building a river discharge prediction model for rivers with available gauge data (true observations). Readers are referred to Kratzert et al. [9] for methods of dealing with ungauged basins. To develop the hybrid model for predicting discharge over an extended period, we utilized the following data sources: (a) RAPID historical discharge predictions for the river of interest (a physics-based approximate model); (b) historical gauge measurement time series data for the river of interest (true values); and (c) runoff data for all rivers within the specified basin.

We perform three primary data processes on the mentioned datasets: (a) We use the Hanning filter to smoothen RAPID model predictions; (b) For $N_{\text{rivers-in-basin}}$ numbers of rivers in the basin of interest and $N_{\text{total-days}}$ number of days for which runoff data is available, the dimension of the runoff data is typically very large $N_{\text{rivers-in-basin}} \times N_{\text{total-days}}$. Since there is a correlation in the runoff of rivers within the same watershed (neighborhood effect), we apply Singular Value Decomposition (SVD) to reduce the dimensions of the runoff dataset; (c) To further reduce the dimensionality of all three datasets, we downsample the number of days when the machine learning (ML) method selected for building the hybrid model deems it necessary.

To build the hybrid ML predictive model, we deployed two different algorithms. The first is Delta Learning, which involves three major steps: (a) training a surrogate for RAPID that is informed by both past RAPID data and past runoff data, along with forecasted values for the near future available from Noah-MP; (b) using the true discharge value and RAPID surrogate outputs to calculate the error (the delta term) in the enhanced-RAPID predictions relative to the true discharge value; and (c) building an ML model that takes past RAPID data, past runoff data, and future forecasted data to predict the delta term. The ML models developed in the first and third steps can then be used to make discharge predictions in a recurrent manner. More details can be found in Section 3.1 of Zhao et al. [4]. The second algorithm is Data Augmentation, which also involves three steps for training: (a) training a RAPID surrogate similar to the Delta Learning algorithm; (b) although the RAPID surrogate in the previous step was trained on RAPID and runoff data, we obtain the output time series using the RAPID surrogate by replacing the past RAPID data with true discharge values, along with the runoff data, yielding an augmented prediction vector; and (c) finally, using the true discharge data, runoff data, and the augmented prediction vector from the previous step, we train an ML model capable of directly predicting the gauge measurements. More details can be found in Section 3.2 of Zhao et al. [4].

The hybrid ML models were implemented in a basin located in Colorado, consisting of 431 watersheds with a river running through them. Among these 431 watersheds, six have gauges, and these become rivers of interest. Figure 1 illustrates the prediction results for three of these rivers, built using the GP-NARX and Data Augmentation algorithm.

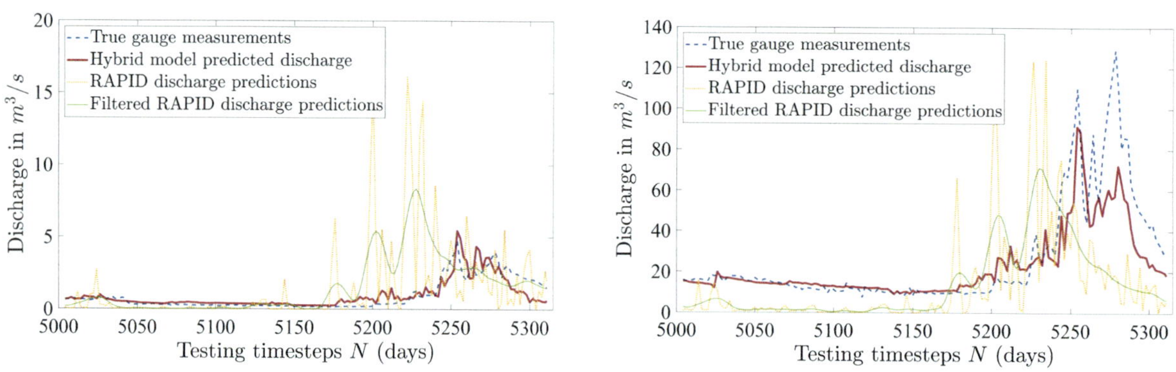

Fig. 1 Discharge prediction using the hybrid ML models: (left) a case of a river with low discharge; (right) a case of a river with high discharge.

In addition to GP-NARX, we have also investigated more complex ML methods such as long short-term memory (LSTM) networks, bidirectional LSTM (Bi-LSTM), and NARX-Net. Readers are referred to Zhao et al. [4] for more details on the implementation, results, and comparative performance of the various ML methods. As part of this ongoing effort, we have also developed the capability to obtain uncertainty bounds in the discharge predictions.

Leveraging Discharge Forecasting Capability to Lifecycle Modeling and Decision-Making

River discharge and gauge height share a direct relationship with the upstream water head (and, by extension, with the downstream head controlled by the dam). Forecasting discharge over an extended period allows for the capture of (a) seasonality in loading (see illustration in Fig. 2); (b) intensity of loading; (c) uncertainty bounds in loading.

In our ongoing research effort, we plan to investigate the use of discharge prediction capabilities in (a) projecting the behavior of the structure in the near future as part of prognostics and RUL estimation; (b) assisting in modeling seasonality for the loading model used in Structural Health Monitoring (SHM) system design and lifecycle optimization; and (c) scheduling operations and maintenance plans. For instance, the seasonality in the discharge, as shown in the figure below, is crucial to include when simulating the structure's lifecycle.

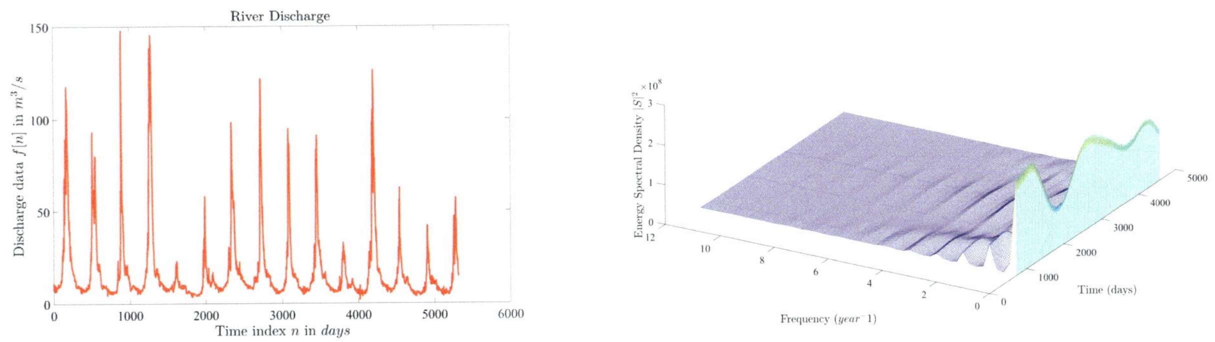

Fig. 2 Seasonality in river discharge: (a) river discharge time series; (b) spectrogram of river discharge data showing annual, semi-annual, and quarterly seasonality.

Other applications in river and asset management include: (a) early warning for flooding and decision-making for dam and miter gate operations; and (b) providing support for dredging operations.

Conclusion

In this brief article, we discussed different algorithms and machine learning methods that are both physics-based and data-driven, which can be used to forecast river discharge more accurately than the currently existing physics-based approximations and for a longer period of time. This capability could have several implications for improving lifecycle simulations of river-based assets where the loading depends on river discharge. In addition, such predictive models can provide early warnings for floods and potentially save lives and property by enabling well-informed operational decisions.

References

1. Yang, Yichao, Mayank Chadha, Zhen Hu, Manuel A. Vega, Matthew D. Parno, and Michael D. Todd. "A probabilistic optimal sensor design approach for structural health monitoring using risk-weighted f-divergence." Mechanical Systems and Signal Processing 161 (2021): 107920.
2. Vega, Manuel A., Zhen Hu, Yichao Yang, Mayank Chadha, and Michael D. Todd. *Diagnosis, prognosis, and maintenance decision making for civil infrastructure: Bayesian data analytics and machine learning*. Springer International Publishing, 2022
3. Zhao, Ying, Mayank Chadha, Nicholas Olsen, Elissa Yeates, Josh Turner, Guga Gugaratshan, Guofeng Qian, Michael D. Todd, and Zhen Hu. "Machine learning-enabled calibration of river routing model parameters." *Journal of Hydroinformatics* 25, no. 5 (2023): 1799–1821.
4. Zhao, Ying, Mayank Chadha, Dakota Barthlow, Elissa M. Yeates, Charles J. Mcknight, Natalie P. Memarsadeghi, Guga Gugaratshan, Michael D. Todd, and Zhen Hu. "Physics-enhanced machine learning models for streamflow discharge forecasting." *Journal of Hydroinformatics* (2024).

5. McCarthy, Gerald T. *The unit hydrograph and flood routing*. Army Engineer District, Providence, 1939.
6. David, Cédric H., David R. Maidment, Guo-Yue Niu, Zong-Liang Yang, Florence Habets, and Victor Eijkhout. "River network routing on the NHDPlus dataset." *Journal of Hydrometeorology* 12, no. 5 (2011): 913–934.
7. David, Cédric H., James S. Famiglietti, Zong-Liang Yang, Florence Habets, and David R. Maidment. "A decade of RAPID—Reflections on the development of an open source geoscience code." *Earth and Space Science* 3, no. 5 (2016): 226–244.
8. Tavakoly, Ahmad A., Alan D. Snow, Cédric H. David, Michael L. Follum, David R. Maidment, and Zong-Liang Yang. "Continental-scale river flow modeling of the Mississippi River Basin using high-resolution NHDPlus dataset." *JAWRA Journal of the American Water Resources Association* 53, no. 2 (2017): 258–279.
9. Kratzert, Frederik, Daniel Klotz, Mathew Herrnegger, Alden K. Sampson, Sepp Hochreiter, and Grey S. Nearing. "Toward improved predictions in ungauged basins: Exploiting the power of machine learning." *Water Resources Research* 55, no. 12 (2019): 11344–11354.

Chapter 5
Experimental Analysis to Enable Low-Latency Structural Health Monitoring for Electronics in High-Rate Dynamic Environments

Ryan Yount, Trotter Roberts, Jacob Dodson, Adriane Moura, and Austin R.J. Downey

Abstract Electronic assemblies subjected to high-rate dynamic environments offer the potential of increased robustness and resilience to mechanical loading if integrated with active feedback mechanisms that respond when damage is present in the system or alter mission outcomes when appropriate. To enable active structural control of electronic assemblies, the rapid detection of mechanical damage is crucial. This study focuses on monitoring an electronic package under a shock and introduces a method for enhancing the durability of printed circuit boards through onboard frequency-based damage detection. The experimental setup is comprised of printed circuit boards equipped with representative electronic packages enhanced with embedded sensing capabilities, subjected to controlled shock tests using a drop tower system. This study details the data acquisition process, Fast Fourier Transform (FFT) implementation on the electronic assembly, and the algorithmic strategies for peak detection and response initiation. The frequency-based damage detection system has the capability to increase the robustness and resilience of systems experiencing shock when combined with a closed-loop control system. In future work, the electronic assembly will be re-designed to autonomously process the resulting vibration data using an FFT computed at the edge to identify a change in the critical frequency components associated with potential damage. This work not only extends the understanding of printed circuit board dynamics under stress but also showcases the practical applications of embedded signal processing to enable enhanced system durability and reliability.

Keywords PCB · Fast fourier transform · Shock mitigation · Embedded signal processing

Introduction

The ability to rapidly detect structural damage in electronic assemblies exposed to high-rate dynamic events is crucial for ensuring reliability and longevity [1]. High-rate dynamic events occur frequently in various contexts, including automotive collisions, and aviation accidents. These high-rate dynamic events, or mechanical shock, are defined as abrupt modifications in force, position, velocity, or acceleration, which induce transient states in the system [2]. Such shocks can lead to rapid and unpredictable responses within the structural integrity of components, making it critical to ensure that systems can recover or adapt in real time. The integration of active feedback mechanisms capable of swiftly detecting and responding to structural damage plays a pivotal role in enhancing the robustness of such systems. These mechanisms employ a network of sensors that continuously monitor the system's state, detecting deviations from normal operation that may indicate damage

Ryan Yount · Trotter Roberts · Austin R.J. Downey
Department of Mechanical Engineering, University of South Carolina, Columbia, SC 29208
e-mail: rjyount@email.sc.edu; tjr7@email.sc.edu; austindowney@sc.edu

Austin R.J. Downey
Department of Civil and Environmental Engineering, University of South Carolina, Columbia, SC 29208
e-mail: austindowney@sc.edu

Jacob Dodson
Air Force Research Laboratory, Eglin AFB, FL 32542
e-mail: jacob.dodson.2@us.af.mil

Adriane Moura
Applied Research Associates Inc, Niceville, FL 32578
e-mail: adriane.moura.ctr@us.af.mil

Thomas Matarazzo et al. (eds.), *Data Science in Engineering, Vol. 11*, Conference Proceedings of the Society for Experimental Mechanics Series, https://doi.org/10.13052/9788743801566-5

or failure. Upon detecting an anomaly, the system can immediately implement corrective actions—such as adjusting loads, altering operational parameters, or rerouting energy flows—thereby preventing further damage. This capability not only mitigates potential failures but also optimizes mission outcomes by adding the possibility of adapting system behavior in response to detected damage [3]. By adapting the system's behavior in response to detected damage, these active feedback mechanisms ensure that mission-critical tasks can continue with minimal interruption. Furthermore, this adaptability reduces the need for redundant system designs and manual intervention, thereby increasing operational efficiency and prolonging the system's lifespan [4]. Electronic packages subjected to shock and vibration must endure rigorous testing to validate their durability under real-world conditions. A useful approach to enhancing structural health is onboard frequency-based damage detection [5]. Traditional methods such as accelerometer-based monitoring for Structural Health Monitoring (SHM) have been extensively studied. Accelerometers are commonly used to capture vibration data and analyze modal characteristics of Printed Circuit Boards (PCBs) under varying mechanical loads [6]. Studies aimed at investigating how PCBs respond to mechanical stresses and dynamic forces contribute valuable insights into understanding how to build more robust electronics [7]. By embedding sensors within PCBs and employing signal processing techniques like Fast Fourier Transforms (FFTs) [8], it becomes feasible to monitor vibration signatures of electronic assemblies during and after shock events. The analysis of frequency components allows for the rapid identification of changes indicative of mechanical damage, enabling response mechanisms to mitigate potential failures.

In shock events, the impact can adversely affect the entire system, highlighting the importance of controlled and repeatable testing methodologies. To address this challenge, shock test systems such as drop towers are used, which simulate abrupt mechanical impacts to evaluate how electronic assemblies withstand sudden forces. These systems provide controlled, repeatable environments that replicate the dynamic stresses encountered during deployment. Dynamic analysis techniques have similarly been applied to investigate the behavior of electronic assemblies under mechanical shock loads. For instance, studies have focused on scenarios such as the dynamic analysis of fixed-fixed beams subjected to mechanical shock, revealing critical insights into the structural response and potential failure modes under high-rate loading conditions [9]. Furthermore, the fundamental principles of SHM have been clarified through comprehensive frameworks and theoretical studies. These include the axioms and foundational concepts that underpin effective SHM practices, guiding the development of robust monitoring strategies aimed at enhancing the reliability and longevity of electronic systems [10]. For electronic feedback, resistive circuits have been employed for continuity measurements in electronic assemblies, facilitating real-time assessment of circuit integrity under dynamic conditions [11]. This method is particularly effective in detecting and diagnosing potential faults promptly, thereby enhancing the reliability of electronic systems in high-stress environments.

Advancements in edge computing present promising avenues for real-time data processing in SHM applications. Edge computing architectures enable data analysis closer to the source, which reduces latency [12] and supports timely decision-making based on monitored parameters [13], particularly in smart electronics applications [14]. This capability is particularly advantageous in SHM, where rapid responses to dynamic events are critical for preemptive maintenance and operational efficiency in electronic assemblies.

This study focuses on the development and implementation of a frequency-based damage detection system for electronic assemblies undergoing shock tests using a drop tower setup. The experimental framework involves equipping PCBs with embedded sensors capable of acquiring the necessary vibration data. An FFT algorithm is employed to extract critical frequency components associated with structural integrity, facilitating rapid assessment of damage. Key aspects of this research include a detailed description of the data acquisition process, the implementation of FFTs on the acquired data, and the algorithmic strategies for peak detection and initiation of response actions. The contribution of this work is the advancement our understanding of PCB dynamics under shock-induced mechanical stresses and introducing the application of embedded signal processing for enhancing durability. This study also contributes to the broader field of structural health monitoring in electronic assemblies. While this study focuses on frequency-based damage detection, the next step will involve developing edge computing frameworks to implement these processes in real-time.

Methodology

To determine the expected modal frequencies of the PCBs under investigation, vibrational simulations were conducted using finite element analysis software. The geometry and boundary conditions used in the simulation are provided in Figure 1. For this experiment, a 5.5 inch PCB was clamped with a pseudo-fixity setup. Since the clamp extended 0.5 inches and was positioned 0.5 inches from the board's edge to provide space for data acquisition wiring, the effective length of the PCB measured from the edge of the clamp to the opposite edge of the board was determined to be 4.5 inches.

The simulations were performed with and without the additional mass attached to the board, aiming to understand the impact of the mass on the board's vibrational characteristics. A frequency analysis was performed to identify the natural

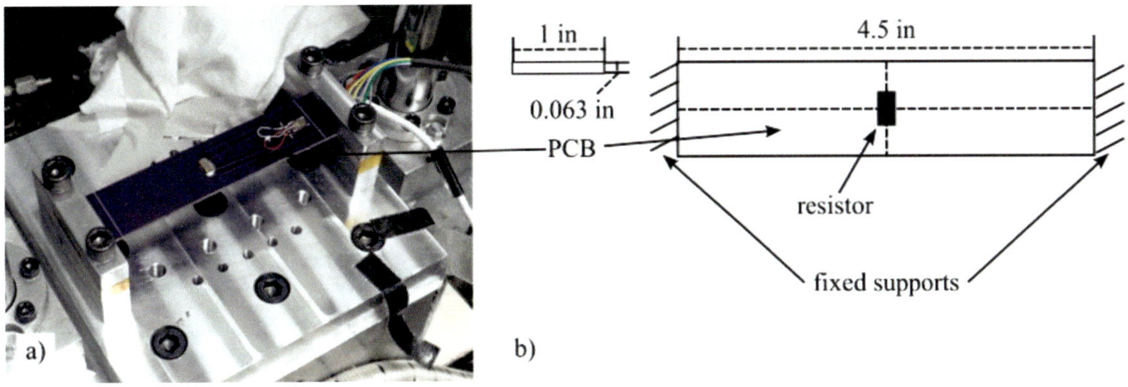

Fig. 1 a. PCB configured in the test setup b. Geometry and boundary conditions created for simulation of the PCB.

frequencies and mode shapes of the PCB as shown in Figure 2. The material properties used in the simulations are shown in Table 1. This analysis was useful in determining expected outcomes for how the board will respond to mechanical shock and the resulting vibrations.

Table 1 Material properties used in the simulations of the PCB

Material	Density (lb/ft^3)	Young's Modulus (psi)	Poisson Ratio
FR4	118.64	2,697,707	0.2

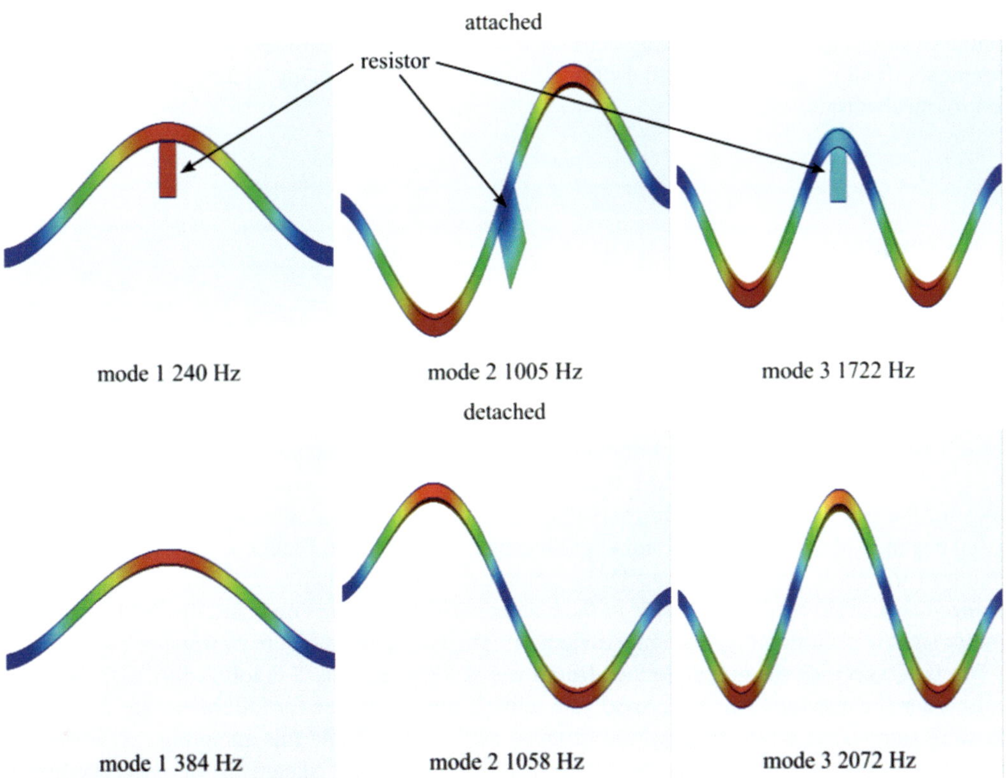

Fig. 2 Simulation results showcasing the mode shapes and frequencies with and without the mass attached.

Notably, the first mode, which is of primary interest in this study, exhibited significant variation depending on the presence of additional mass. With the resistor connected to the board, mode 1 was found to have a frequency of 240 Hz. After the resistor was removed, the frequency of mode 1 increased to 384 Hz.

To enable the detection of mechanical damage in the PCBs, a frequency-based approach utilizing FFTs is employed [5]. This method leverages the inherent vibration signatures of the assemblies captured by the embedded sensors during shock. The FFT algorithm converts the time-domain vibration signal $x(n)$ into the frequency domain $X(f)$, as shown in Equation 1, allowing for the identification of specific frequency components associated with structural integrity. The signal is decomposed into its frequency components using the FFT. Next, the resulting spectrum is normalized by dividing by the number of samples. Lastly, only the positive side of the frequency spectrum is retained, as the FFT output is symmetric for real-valued signals.

$$X(f) = \sum_{n=0}^{N-1} x(n)e^{-j2\pi fn/N} \tag{1}$$

where $x(n)$ represents the sampled time-domain signal, N is the number of samples, and f is the frequency.

Algorithmic strategies for peak detection can be implemented on edge computing devices to provide more rapid damage assessment. Such algorithms are designed to analyze FFT-transformed data and identify significant peaks or changes in critical frequency components. As damage occurs, a shift in the modal frequencies is expected. Some strategies include threshold-based peak detection, pattern recognition, and adaptive filtering.

To implement edge computing for rapid damage assessment on the PCBs, several important factors must be considered. A suitable microcontroller capable of handling real-time signal processing tasks should be chosen. This microcontroller must be able to connect to all of the sensors in the system and have a high enough sampling rate to capture the vibration signals of interest. An algorithm to perform and read an FFT on the captured data must be deployed on the microcontroller. Other traits of interest would be a program to trigger a control response such as damping the system when vibrations exceed a threshold and wirelessly transmitting data to an external monitoring system.

While not implemented in this study, the integration of an edge processing device with the damage detection approach enables the implementation of a closed-loop control system. This system would monitor real-time vibration data processed on the edge and could initiate control decisions to mitigate mechanical vibrations when deemed critical. This approach could enhance the resilience of electronic assemblies by actively managing mechanical loads and optimizing performance under dynamic environments. It showcases the potential of edge computing in enhancing system durability through responsive, autonomous control mechanisms.

Experimental Procedure

The experimental setup utilizes a drop tower system to subject electronic packages to controlled shock events. This system, as shown in Figure 3, simulates abrupt mechanical impacts to assess the resilience of the assemblies under dynamic conditions. Controlled impacts allow for systematic evaluation of how electronic components respond to sudden forces, which is crucial for understanding their durability in high-rate dynamic environments.

The electronic packages under test were configured as 4.5-inch PCBs clamped as a fixed-fixed beam. Each PCB is equipped with a piezoresistive accelerometer, two strain gauges, and a resistor acting as a mass setup in a resistive circuit. This setup allows for the precise detection of impacts that cause the mass to fall, thereby indicating the onset of structural failure. A close-up example of the PCB before and after detachment is shown in Figure 4.

The integration of the shock test system and DAQ facilitated rapid data analysis during testing. The data acquisition process synchronized an accelerometer on the base of the hammer with the sensors on board the PCB for accurate correlation of input and output signals. Additionally, a voltage divider circuit, as shown in Figure 5, was used to monitor the integrity of the resistor. The DAQ recorded the output voltage from the circuit, which was 2.5 volts while the resistor was intact and dropped to 0 volts when the resistor detached, providing a reliable time reference for failure events.

The signals were sampled at a rate of 2 million samples per second. While this sampling rate is significantly higher than necessary, it ensured precise data capture and avoided aliasing. A high-speed camera was used in conjunction with the DAQ to visually capture the precise moment of damage initiation on the PCBs, as shown in Figure 6. This visual cue was a supplement of sensor data, enhancing the understanding of failure mechanisms under high-rate conditions.

After each test, the clamps holding the PCBs were torqued to 15 in lbs to standardize test conditions as each clamped end simulated a fixed support. Testing sequences ranged from lower to higher gravity (g) shocks, systematically increasing impact intensity to gather comprehensive data points before observing failure. An example of how the shock propagated throughout the PCB is shown in Figure 7.

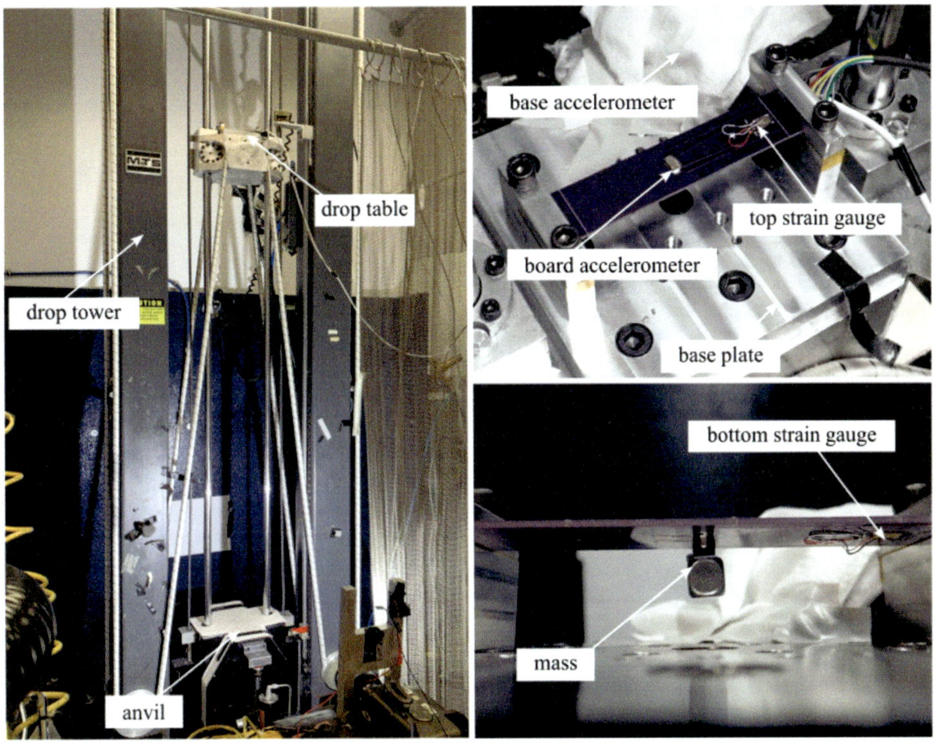

Fig. 3 Drop tower test setup including the top and bottom of the fixed-fixed PCB.

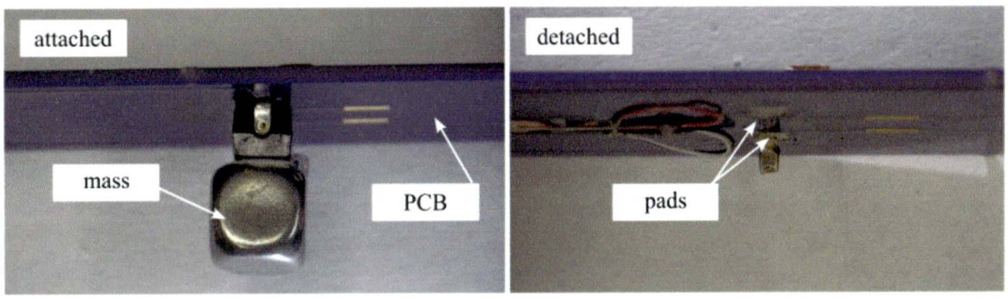

Fig. 4 Close view of the PCB being tested before and after the mass was detached.

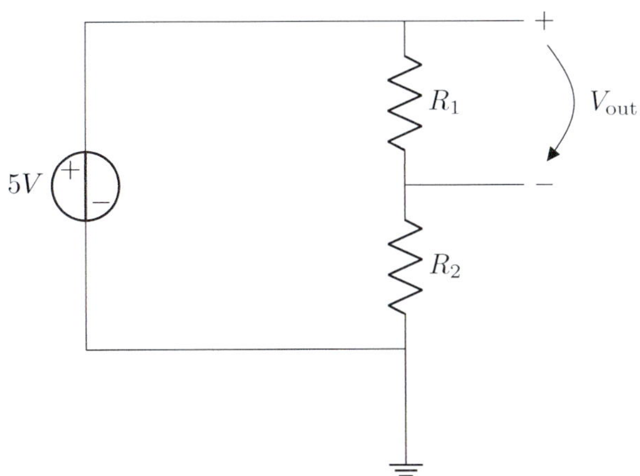

Fig. 5 Voltage divider circuit used in the experiment to read from the PCB resistor.

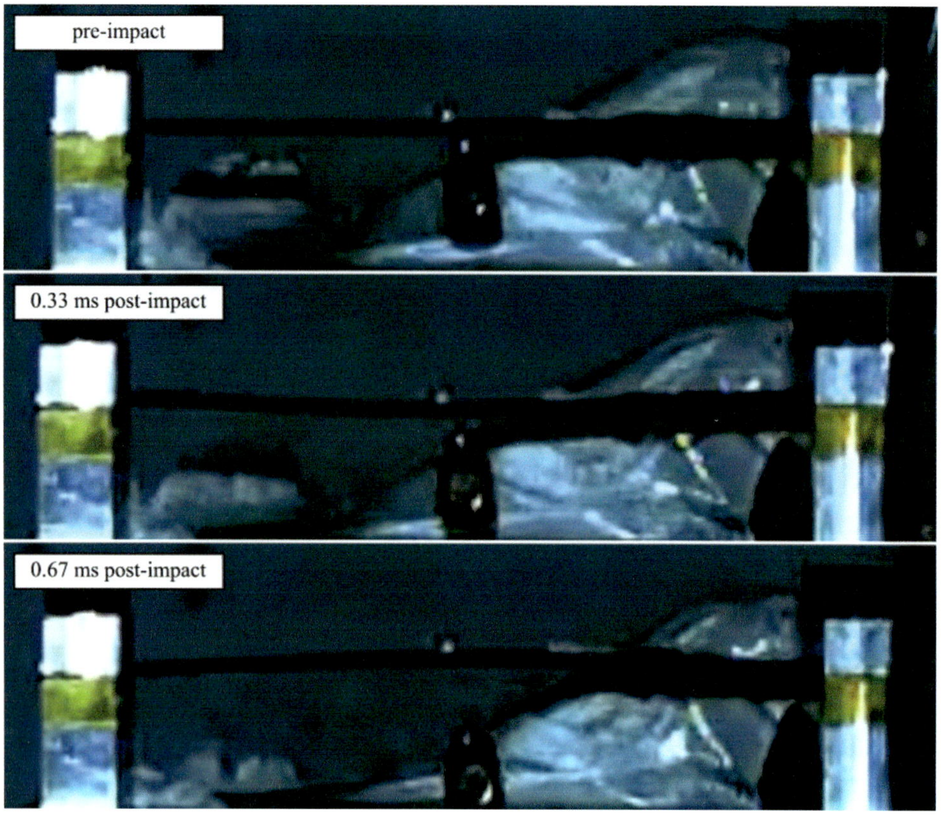

Fig. 6 Frames from a high-speed camera showing the board during a resistor failure drop.

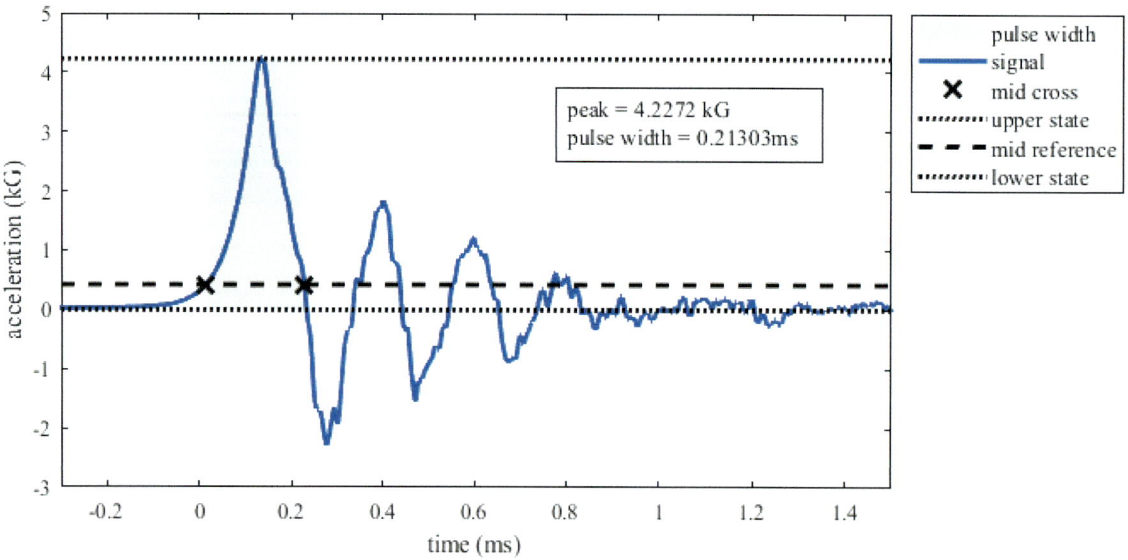

Fig. 7 Analysis of a time domain signal from the accelerometer on the board during a shock test.

Results and Discussion

The experimental data acquired from the shock tests, published in a public repository [15], revealed significant findings regarding the effect of the resistor circuit under stress conditions. Across multiple trials, the provided DC voltage to the resistor circuit stayed relatively constant until a shock occurred where the mass fell. A comparison of time domain signals to assess the behavior of the PCB during the failure test was plotted in Figure 8. Some differences are shown during the response, which can be attributed to sequential excitations due to the detached component colliding with the board.

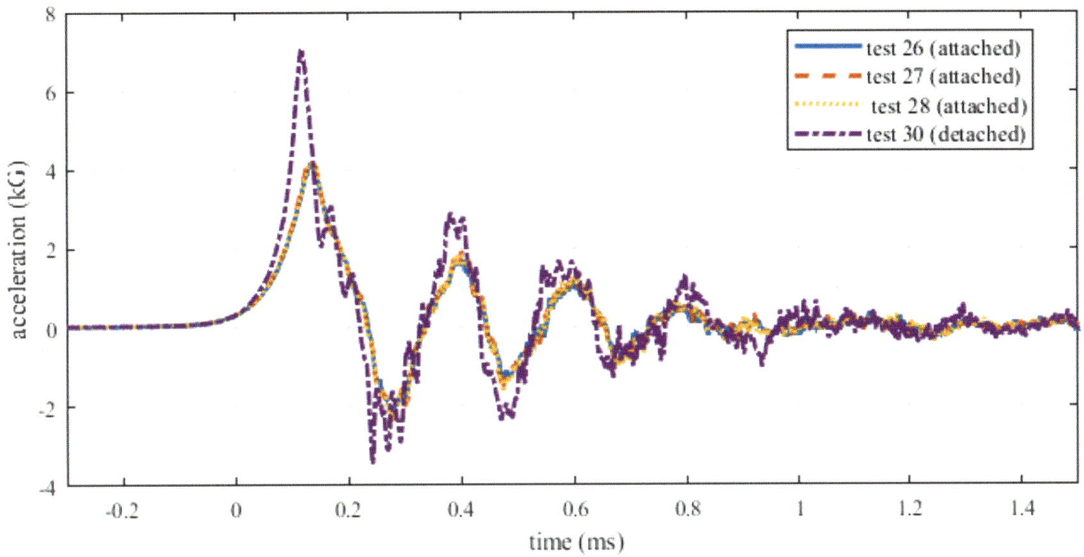

Fig. 8 Time series representation of shock tests leading up to a final test where the resistor became detached.

The Fourier analysis conducted on each test indicated pronounced alterations in the frequency signatures of the boards following the mass detachment, as shown in Figure 9. Specifically, when observing the first modal frequency, there was a significant change in line with the change expected from simulations. In Table 2, an analysis of the difference between the frequencies seen in the tested data and the frequencies expected from the simulations is shown.

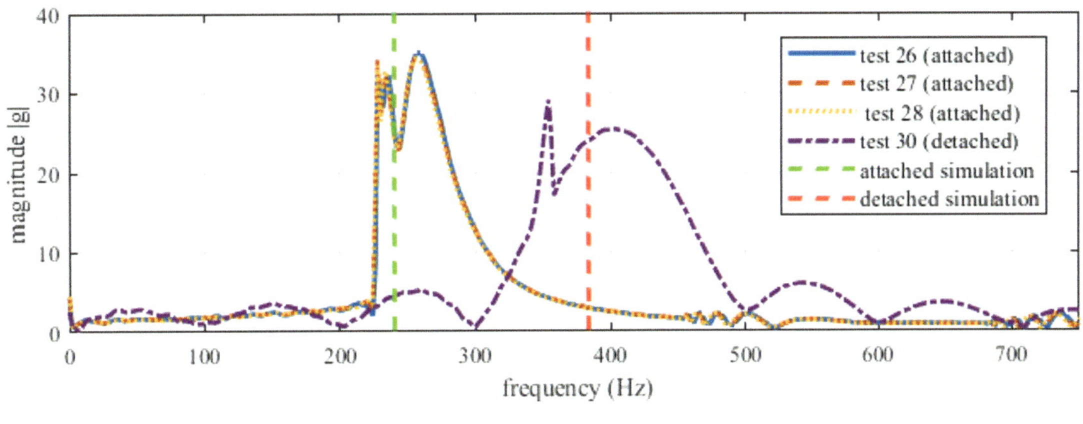

Fig. 9 Sequential Fourier transforms from shock tests until the resistor becomes detached.

Table 2 Error analysis of the frequencies seen from the simulations and the tested data

Condition	Simulated Frequency (Hz)	Tested Frequency (Hz)	Absolute Error (Hz)	Percentage Error (%)
With resistor	240	258	18	7.50
Without resistor	384	354	30	7.81

This analysis highlights the impact of circuit failure on the electrical signal's spectral content, underscoring the feasibility of rapid damage detection using frequency analysis.

Conclusion

This study demonstrates the effectiveness of frequency-based damage detection using FFTs in identifying mechanical damage in electronic assemblies subjected to high-rate dynamic environments. The notable frequency changes observed upon the occurrence of damage highlight the viability of this method for enhancing SHM in such scenarios.

Integrating edge computing into the damage detection process offers several potential benefits. By processing FFT-transformed data locally on edge devices, the system can achieve rapid detection of damage events. This capability reduces latency in decision-making and lays a foundation for implementing responsive control strategies to mitigate mechanical vibrations before they lead to failures.

Future research on this project will include a multi-faceted approach including the implementation of an edge computing device, the optimization of sensor placements, the development of more advanced simulation models, and the integration of these processes with usual packing practices used to mitigate shock.

This paper establishes the foundation for the future development of edge computing architectures, which will enable the autonomous detection of structural changes in real-time. While this work successfully demonstrates frequency-based damage detection, the implementation of closed-loop control using edge devices will be pursued in subsequent studies.

Acknowledgments This material is based upon work supported by the National Science Foundation grant numbers 1937535, 1956071 and 2237696 with additional support from the Air Force Office of Scientific Research (AFOSR) through award no. FA9550-21-1-0083. Any opinions, findings conclusions, or recommendations expressed in this material are those of the authors and do not necessarily reflect the views of the National Science Foundation, or the United States Air Force. (Distribution A. Approved for public release; distribution unlimited (AFRL-2024-5024)).

References

1. Lalanne, C. *Mechanical Shock*. CRC Press, 1st edition (2002)
2. Dodson, J., Downey, A., Laflamme, S., Todd, M.D., Moura, A.G., Wang, Y., Mao, Z., Avitabile, P., and Blasch, E. *High-Rate Structural Health Monitoring and Prognostics: An Overview*, pages 213–217. Springer International Publishing (2021)
3. Song, Z.G., Li, F.M., and Zhang, W. "Active flutter and aerothermal postbuckling control for nonlinear composite laminated panels in supersonic airflow". *Journal of Intelligent Material Systems and Structures*, 26(7):840–857 (2014)
4. Chomette, B., Chesné, S., Rémond, D., and Gaudiller, L. "Damage reduction of on-board structures using piezoelectric components and active modal control—application to a printed circuit board". *Mechanical Systems and Signal Processing*, 24(2):352–364 (2010)
5. Downey, A. and Micheli, L. "Vibration mechanics: A practical introduction for mechanical, civil, and aerospace engineers" (2024)
6. *Health Monitoring of PCB's Under Mechanical Shock Loads*, volume ASME 2019 International Technical Conference and Exhibition on Packaging and Integration of Electronic and Photonic Microsystems of *International Electronic Packaging Technical Conference and Exhibition* (2019)
7. Jalink, J., Roucou, R., Zaal, J.J.M., Lesventes, J., and Rongen, R.T.H. "Effect of pcb and package type on board level vibration using vibrational spectrum analysis". In *2017 IEEE 67th Electronic Components and Technology Conference (ECTC)*, pages 470–475 (2017)
8. Yount, R., Satme, J.N., Wamai, D., and Downey, A.R.J. "Edge processing for frequency identification on drone-deployed structural health monitoring sensor nodes". In Muench, P.L., Nguyen, H.G., and Diltz, R., editors, *Unmanned Systems Technology XXVI*, page 25. SPIE (2024)
9. Sharma, G., Mishra, A., and Selvaraj, P. "Dynamic analysis of fixed-fixed beam under mechanical shock loads". *IOP Conference Series: Materials Science and Engineering*, 998(1):012019 (2020)
10. Worden, K., Farrar, C.R., Manson, G., and Park, G. "The fundamental axioms of structural health monitoring". *Proceedings of the Royal Society A: Mathematical, Physical and Engineering Sciences*, 463(2082):1639–1664 (2007)
11. Aytekin, B. "Vibration analysis of pcbs and electronic components". Master's thesis, Middle East Technical University (2008)
12. Kabir, E., Coble, D., Satme, J.N., Downey, A.R., Bakos, J.D., Andrews, D., and Huang, M. "Accelerating lstm-based high-rate dynamic system models". In *2023 33rd International Conference on Field-Programmable Logic and Applications (FPL)*, volume 10, pages 327–332. IEEE (2023)
13. Wang, X., Han, Y., Leung, V.C.M., Niyato, D., Yan, X., and Chen, X. *Fundamentals of Edge Computing*, pages 15–32. Springer Singapore, Singapore (2020)
14. Krishnasamy, E., Varrette, S., and Mucciardi, M. "Edge computing: An overview of framework and applications". Technical report (December 2020). https://prace-ri.eu/wp-content/uploads/Edge-Computing-An-Overview-of-Framework-and-Applications.pdf
15. Yount, R., Dodson, J., and Moura, A. "Dataset 9 repeated impact testing of rectangular electronic assembly"

Chapter 6
Fast-TDA Implementation for High Rate Dynamic Systems in Noisy Environment and Introduction to Chaotic System

Arman Razmarashooli, Daniel A. Salazar Martinez, Simon Laflamme, Chao Hu, Paul T. Schrader, Gurcan Comert, Negash Begashaw, and Jacob Dodson

Abstract High-rate systems (HRS), defined as engineering systems experiencing substantial disturbances/variability over short periods of time, can be significantly empowered by implementing feedback mechanisms, but these mechanisms are severely impeded by the complexity of the high-rate dynamics and tight reaction time constraints. In particular, the HRS time scale is constrained to 1 ms for whole closed-loop mechanism, including data acquisition, assessment execution, and decision-making. A compelling tool to analyze complex dynamic systems is topological data analysis (TDA). Yet, TDA requires a high computational cost and is not applicable to the HRS time scale. Here, the authors introduce the concept of *Fast-TDA*. Fast-TDA is a set of computationally efficient algorithms constructed to extract TDA-inspired features from time series for targeting HRS analytics. This study investigates methods mimicking the capabilities of persistent homology (PH) to extract the topological characteristics of one-dimensional (H_1) voids for dynamic systems embedded in two dimensions. This pseudo-PH process dynamically fits the phase space point cloud with ellipses using a peak identification method and fitting error analysis, subsequently identifying intersections between the ellipses. This approach is demonstrated on synthetic datasets embedded in two dimensions with added noise and the Lorenz attractor. Results show that Fast-TDA can accurately extract key topological features in noisy and chaotic environments over comparative state-of-the-art TDA methods.

Keywords High rate dynamic systems · Topological data analysis · Persistent homology · Chaotic systems · Lorenz attractor

Arman Razmarashooli · Daniel A. Salazar Martinez · Simon Laflamme
Department of Civil, Construction, and Environmental Engineering, Iowa State University, Ames, IA 50011
e-mail: shooli@iastate.edu; daniel94@iastate.edu; laflamme@iastate.edu

Simon Laflamme
Department of Electrical and Compu ter Engineering, Iowa State University, Ames, IA 50011
e-mail: laflamme@iastate.edu

Chao Hu
Department of Mechanical Engineering, University of Connecticut, Storrs, CT 06269
e-mail: chao.hu@uconn.edu

Paul T. Schrader
Air Force Research Laboratory, Information Directorate, Rome, NY 13441
e-mail: paul.schrader.1@us.af.mil

Gurcan Comert
School of Science and Engineering, Benedict College, Columbia, SC 29204
e-mail: gurcan.comert@benedict.edu

Negash Begashaw
Department of Computational Data Science and Engineering, North Carolina A&T State University, Greensboro, NC 27411
e-mail: negash.begashaw@benedict.edu

Jacob Dodson
Air Force Research Laboratory, Munitions Directorate, Eglin AFB, FL 32542
e-mail: jacob.dodson.2@us.af.mil

Thomas Matarazzo et al. (eds.), *Data Science in Engineering, Vol. 11*, Conference Proceedings of the Society for Experimental Mechanics Series, https://doi.org/10.13052/9788743801566-6

Introduction

Topological data analysis (TDA) is a fast-growing field that leverages algebraic topology and modern mathematics to analyze the shape of data sets [1]. TDA's primary goal is finding topological features such as connected components, loops, and voids, etc., in data by constructing *simplicial complexes* from point clouds [2]. These simplicial complexes are multi-dimensional forms of *graphs* that capture the local relationships between data points [1] while simultaneously inheriting the topology of its underlying data set. TDA is particularly useful for analyzing complex, noisy datasets. Persistent homology (PH) algebraically represents how topological features (multi-dimensional holes) in a dataset change over different scales. Thus, the 0th dimension of PH, or H_0, captures the connected components of a data set, the 1st dimension of PH, or H_1, captures the 1-dimensional (1D) holes of a data set, the 2nd dimension of PH, or H_2, captures the 2D holes or voids of a data set, etc. For instance, assuming a two-dimensional point cloud, a circle of diameter $\epsilon > 0$ is drawn around each point and the diameter of the circles dilates for all time. As the diameters grow, points connect when the edges of two circles overlap [3]. The connected points may eventually form loops or one-dimensional holes (birth), which eventually close (death). This process, known as a *filtration* measures, tracks, and records a given data's topological features lifespans as ordered pairs $(birth, death) = (b, d)$ in high fidelity, and the difference between these times, known as *persistence*, helps us to understand the stability of the features within the data. the results are often visualized in a persistence diagram, which provides insight into the dataset's overall structure, such as periodicity and clustering [3].

In many real applications, data that are collected from systems are time-dependent and represented as time series $\mathbf{x}(t) = [x_1, x_2, \cdots, x_m]$. To apply TDA to time series, it must first be converted into a point cloud. This conversion is typically done using Taken's embedding theorem, which reconstructs the state space of a system from its time series data [4, 5]. By creating a delay vector with an optimally chosen dimension d and time delay τ $\boldsymbol{\chi}(t) = [\mathbf{x}(t), \mathbf{x}(t-\tau), \mathbf{x}(t-2\tau), \cdots, \mathbf{x}(t-(d-1)\tau)]$, one can represent the current state of the system and its past values, createing a point cloud embedded in finite dimensional Euclidean space that preserves the underlying dynamics of the original system topologically equivalent manifold of the same dimension [6, 7]. The embedding dimension d (number of past values to include) and time delay τ (the gap between the successive values) are key parameters typically are chosen by false nearest neighbor test and mutual information methodologies [5]. Once this transformation is complete, TDA can be applied to the embedded data to extract topological invariants. TDA captures key system features by using Taken's embedding theorem. Persistent homology and simplicial complexes are the main tools to find these features. Previous studies have demonstrated that combining TDA features with machine learning algorithms is effective for solving classification problems in various fields, including electrocardiogram classification, time series analysis, and the exploration of large datasets in biology and chemistry [8, 9].

The application domain of this paper is high-rate systems (HRS), defined as dynamic systems experiencing accelerations greater than 100 g_n for durations under 100 milliseconds, such as those found in blast mitigation, advanced weaponry, and hypersonic vehicles [10]. HRS could greatly benefit from feedback systems to ensure optimal operations, but the complexity of their dynamics combined with the tight time constraint complicates the integration of any closed-loop mechanism. This paper investigates the applicability of TDA for real-time state estimation of HRS. TDA features have shown promise for state estimation in such systems, particularly when used as inputs to Gated Neural Networks [11]. However, the computational burden of forming simplicial complexes and persistent diagrams limits TDA's real-time applicability, especially in systems with high sampling rates and chaotic environments. Any closed-loop mechanisms applicable to HRS must function under 1 ms [12]. As a result, the scalability of TDA scalability in high-rate systems becomes a significant obstacle [13]. To address these challenges, we study the concept of *Fast-TDA*, a method inspired by traditional TDA but optimized for efficiency. Fast-TDA avoids the computational cost of constructing simplicial complexes by using geometric methods to extract one-dimensional homology features (H_1) through inscribed ellipses and intersections. This approach not only reduces computational time but also enhances the robustness of feature extraction, particularly in noisy environments.

The rest of the paper is organized as follows. The next section describes the Fast-TDA algorithm to estimate H_1. Following that, we present the synthetic and laboratory datasets used in validating the algorithm. The subsequent section discusses the results, and the final section provides the conclusion.

Algorithm

Our approach uses TDA to determine the birth and death of topological features without relying on constructing a simplicial complex filtration. We focus on analyzing two-dimensional (2D) point clouds. In Fast-TDA, we estimate the persistence of the feature H_1 by first calculating the average distance between neighboring points to determine the birth time. Then, we fit an ellipse through the point cloud, the length of the ellipse's whose minor axis corresponds to the death time of H_1. Various techniques exist to fit one ellipse through a set of points; we adopt the least squares method for ellipse fitting. To account for the nonstationarity in our system, we used a sliding window to extract local features, assuming the system remains stationary within each window [11]. The window is defined to include one period of the system $w_1 = 1/f_{min} + \tau$ where f_{min} represents the system's minimum frequency, ensuring the point cloud forms a loop that corresponds to H_1. However, the problem becomes more complicated when there is more than one frequency in the system since the point cloud should be fitted by multiple ellipses. We investigate dynamic ellipse identification extracted by using a second sliding window nested within the first window. As the first sliding window moves along the time series, the second sliding window with the size of $w_2 = 1/f_{max} + \tau$ where f_{max} represents the system's maximum frequency, captures all inner ellipses. When the fitted error for the ellipses reaches a local minimum, it has found a fitted ellipse. Once the ellipses are fitted/captured in both cases. The intersection of pairs of ellipses are calculated by simultaneously solving their parametric equations.

The objective is to find the set of points where both ellipses overlap, which involves determining if the boundary of one ellipse lies inside the other. In cases where ellipses do not directly intersect but overlap geometrically, the space between the outer boundary of the smaller ellipse and the inner boundary of the larger one is also included as part of the overlap. The regions are combined into a unified composite shape that represents all areas where multiple ellipses overlap. This is achieved by taking the union of the previously identified intersection areas with any new ellipses introduced into the system. The process carefully retains only the portions of the ellipses that are common between them, ensuring that the composite region accurately reflects the overlapping areas. By continuously updating this composite region as new ellipses are added, the system maintains a comprehensive map of all the overlaps between ellipses within the time series. To analyze the properties of the overlapping regions, the largest inscribed circle is computed for each intersection. This is done by evaluating the distance from points inside the region to the boundary and identifying the point that maximizes this distance. The radius of the largest inscribed circle is determined by the distance between this central point and the nearest boundary, ensuring the circle fits entirely within the region without extending beyond it. To optimize this process, a *Voronoi diagram* is employed, where each Voronoi vertex provides a candidate for the circle's center [14]. The vertex with the maximum distance to the boundary is selected, and the corresponding circle is inscribed within the region, revealing the largest possible enclosed area within the overlapping ellipses.

Datasets

To investigate the efficiency and sensitivity of the algorithm in noisy and chaotic environments, three datasets are selected.

Dropbear: The DROPBEAR testbed was developed to validate state estimation algorithms for HRS. As shown in Figure 1, this testbed consists of a cantilever beam subjected to a fast-moving boundary condition using a moving roller [15]. The moving roller has been used to model a sudden change in the beam's stiffness. DROPBEAR can be simplified as a cantilever beam of variable length. The beam typically experiences free vibration and it can be simplified to [11].

$$x(t) = A\cos(wt) + n_p = A\cos(2\pi ft) + n_p \tag{1}$$

where $x(t)$ is the vertical acceleration at the tip, A is the amplitude, f is the natural cyclic frequency in Hertz (Hz), t is time in seconds, and n_p is noise. In the context of free vibration, the fundamental frequency of the beam can be estimated by using Equation 2 [16]:

$$f = \frac{E}{L^2} \tag{2}$$

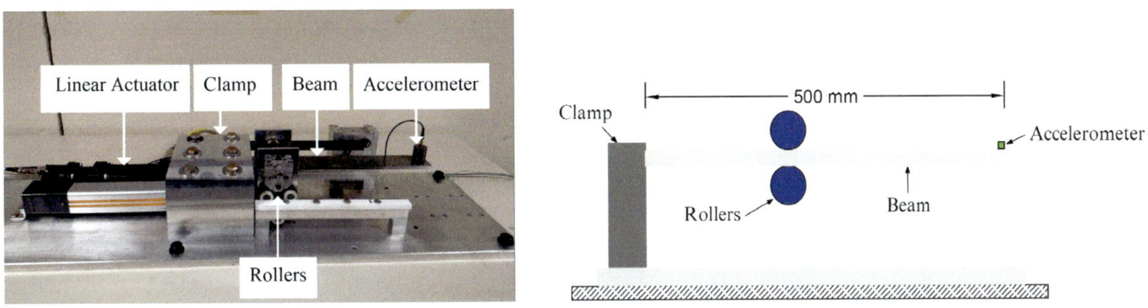

Fig. 1 Picture of the DROPBEAR testbed [11]

where E is a constant and L is length of the beam. Literature has shown that the ideal embedding dimension of a single harmonic signal is 2 [17]. This results in a 2-dimensional point cloud, from which a persistence diagram can be generated, containing information about connected components or zero-dimensional holes, known as the TDA persistent homology (PH) feature representation H_0, and loops or one-dimensional holes, known as TDA PH feature representation H_1.

Chaotic system: To explore chaotic behavior, we use the Lorenz system, a well-known set of ordinary differential equations (ODEs) that exhibits chaos under specific conditions [6]. The system is defined by the following equations:

$$\frac{dx}{dt} = \sigma(y - x) \tag{3}$$

$$\frac{dy}{dt} = x(\rho - z) - y \tag{4}$$

$$\frac{dz}{dt} = xy - \beta z \tag{5}$$

Here, σ, ρ, and β are parameters that influence the system's dynamics. For this study, we set $\sigma = 10$, $\rho = 28$, and $\beta = 8/3$ to induce chaotic behavior. The system is solved numerically, starting from the initial condition $X_0 = [0, 1, 1.05]$, which sets the values for $x(t)$, $y(t)$, and $z(t)$ at $t = 0$. The integration is performed over a time span with 4000 points to accurately capture the system's dynamics. The result is a numerical solution that reflects the chaotic nature of the Lorenz system, providing a time series for $x(t)$ (as shown in Figure 3, and 4).

After obtaining the numerical solution, Taken's embedding theorem is applied to reconstruct the phase space in two dimensions using a time delay of $\tau = 0.1$ seconds [18]. This approach helps in properly unfolding the system's dynamics, effectively capturing the characteristic 'butterfly effect' of the Lorenz attractor.

Synthetic dual harmonic signal: Due to the unavailability of a realistic laboratory dataset, we consider the dual harmonic signal with noise, which is expressed as follows:

$$x(t) = \cos(2\pi f_1 t) + \cos(2\pi f_2 t) + n_p \tag{6}$$

where f_1 and f_2 represents the system's frequencies, with $f_1 > f_2$, and n_p represents noise. The system is embedded using a time delay of $\tau = 0.01$. To ensure that the point cloud consists of multiple ellipses, the time delay must be less than $\tau < 0.25/f_2$. The point cloud is plotted using arbitrary values of f_1 = 3.65 Hz and f_2 = 1.9 Hz to increase the complexity.

Results

In this section, we investigate how well the minor axis in the fitted ellipse can be utilized to find the right cart location compared to maximum persistence and short time Fourier transform (STFT). Data obtained from Fast-TDA, TDA, and STFT are post-processed to map results to the cart location by assuming a quadratic relationship in Equation 2. We conduct the following linear regression.

$$x^2 = a_0 + a_1 F_i \tag{7}$$

where x is the cart location in millimeters (mm), a_0 and a_1 are regression parameters estimated using a least squares estimator, and F_i is the feature obtained from Fast-TDA (the minor axis), TDA (the maximum persistence of H_1), and STFT (the frequency of the system). Table 1 lists regression parameters for various features. Results indicate that Fast-TDA provides a better estimation of the cart location relative to TDA based on the value of R^2. The DROPBEAR test corresponds to Dataset 2 [19]. The dataset contains three distinct cart movement patterns, each with different velocities and accelerations. For better comparison, the results were divided into three sections: Section 1 covers the cart movement from 0.7 seconds to 17.8 seconds, Section 2 from 17.8 seconds to 32.5 seconds, and Section 3 from 32.5 seconds to 41.8 seconds. Data is embedded using $\tau = 0.0008$ seconds, and the size of the moving window is $w = 0.025$ seconds.

Table 1 Results from LSE

Method	a_0	a_1	R^2
TDA	-0.92	2.47	0.87
STFT	-0.034	0.93	0.95
Fast-TDA	0.46	2.16	0.91

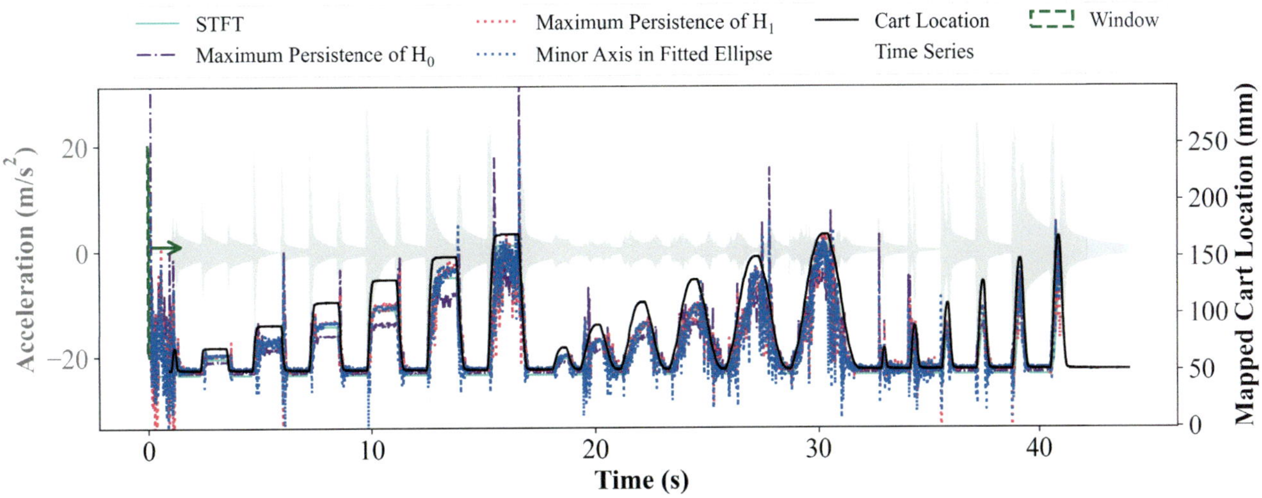

Fig. 2 Cart localization results on DROPBEAR using various features

We evaluate performance through three performance metrics (J_1, J_2, and J_3) [11]. Metric J_1 is the mean absolute error between the actual cart location and the mapped cart location for each section of the excitation. Metric $J_{2,i}$ is the number of instances over the signal that the estimation does not remain below a given distance i (in mm, here taken as $i = 5, 10$, and 20 mm, with 20 mm arbitrarily taken as an acceptable target). Metric $J_{3,i}$ is the mean absolute error of the cart location when the estimated cart position is within the given distance i (in mm). Figure 2 plots the time series results of the car localization using various features. Table 2 list results in terms of performance metrics A study of the metrics shows that, in terms of J_1, Fast-TDA performs similar to TDA in section 3, but outperform TDA in the other sections. However, STFT outperforms both Fast-TDA and TDA in sections 1 and 2. Metric J_2 demonstrates that Fast-TDA accurately maps within 20 mm of the correct cart location over 90% of the time, outperforming TDA in all cases. It also performs similarly to the SFTF or even better, except notably under J_3.

We analyze the performance of windowing as a pre-defined hyperparameter in both TDA and Fast-TDA for chaotic behavior, as the correct window size in such systems is generally unknown. The study is conducted using four different window sizes. Figures 3 and 4 show the time series for $x(t)$ and the evolution of various window sizes for TDA and Fast-TDA. It can be observed that a window size of 1.5 seconds produces the most stable results, with performance deteriorating as the window size decreases, becoming unstable at 0.5 seconds. In contrast, results in Figure 4 indicate that Fast-TDA performs similarly for window sizes of 1 and 1.5 seconds. Although there is some instability with the smaller window sizes, Fast-TDA maintains the trend with increased noise. The results suggest that Fast-TDA is less sensitive to window size compared to TDA.

Lastly, we examine the sensitivity of Fast-TDA and TDA results in noisy environments. Results for both noise-free and noisy dual harmonic signals are plotted in Figures 5 and 6. Figure 5 (a) and 6 (a) shows the time series and sliding windows,

Table 2 Performance results for cart localization on DROPBEAR.

Section	Method	J_1 (mm)	$J_{2,5}$ (%)	$J_{2,10}$ (%)	$J_{2,20}$ (%)	$J_{3,5}$ (mm)	$J_{3,10}$ (mm)	$J_{3,20}$ (mm)
Section 1	TDA	8.7	46	29	12	1.4	2.9	4.9
	STFT	6.3	38	13	3	3.4	4.6	5.4
	Fast-TDA	8.3	42	30	10	1.9	4.6	5.0
Section 2	TDA	10.2	56	34	15	1.9	3.8	6.0
	STFT	7.3	50	23	6	3.5	4.6	6.4
	Fast-TDA	9.2	54	31	11	2.1	3.9	6.2
Section 3	TDA	5.7	30	18	8	1.3	2.1	3.4
	STFT	5.9	21	12	5	4	4.4	5.1
	Fast-TDA	5.7	28	17	7	1.9	2.6	3.8

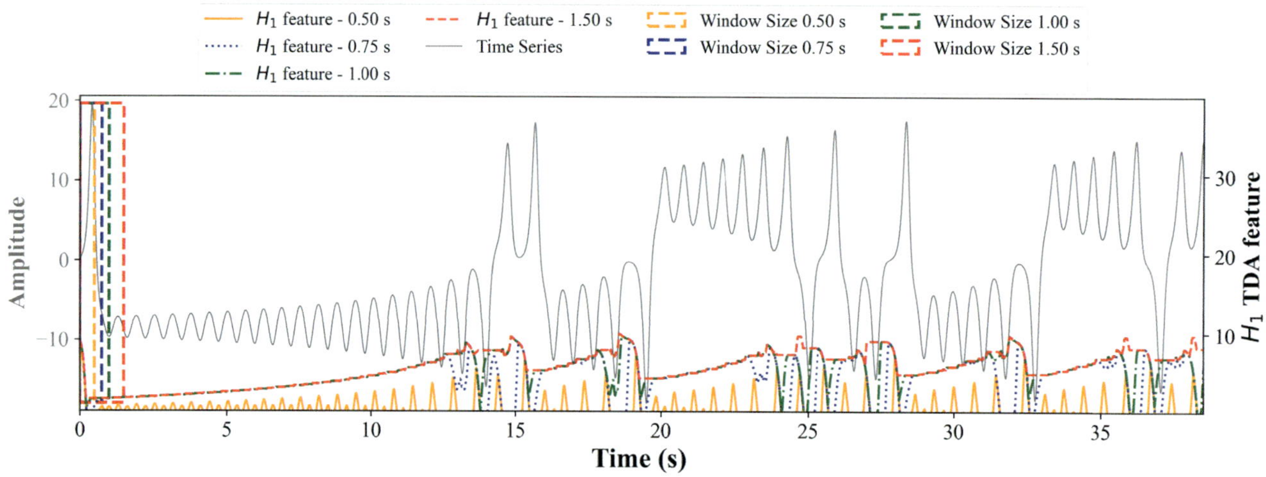

Fig. 3 TDA feature evolution on Lorenz system under various window sizes.

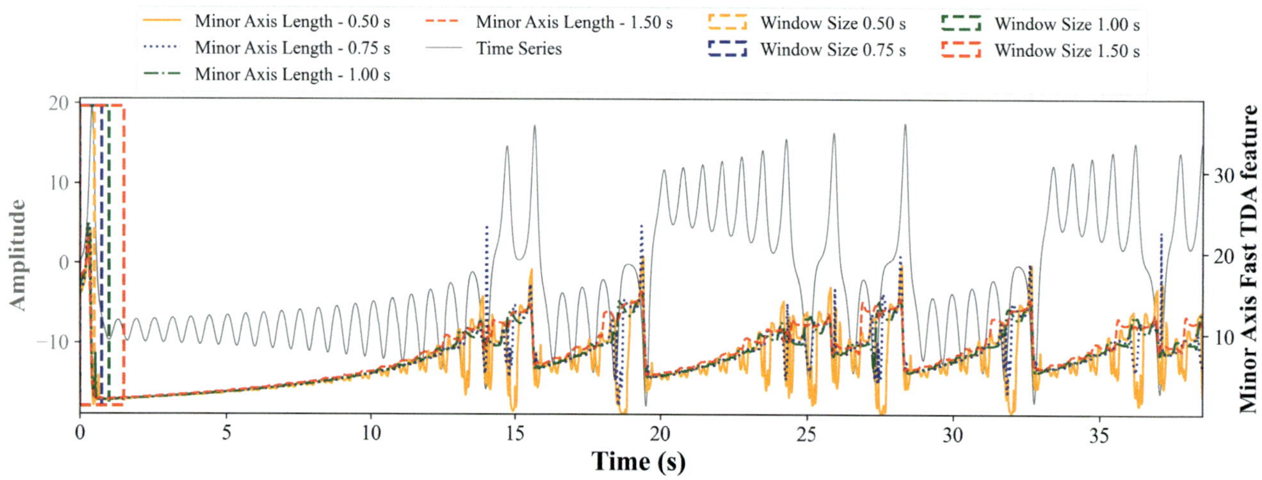

Fig. 4 Fast-TDA feature evolution on Lorenz system under various window sizes.

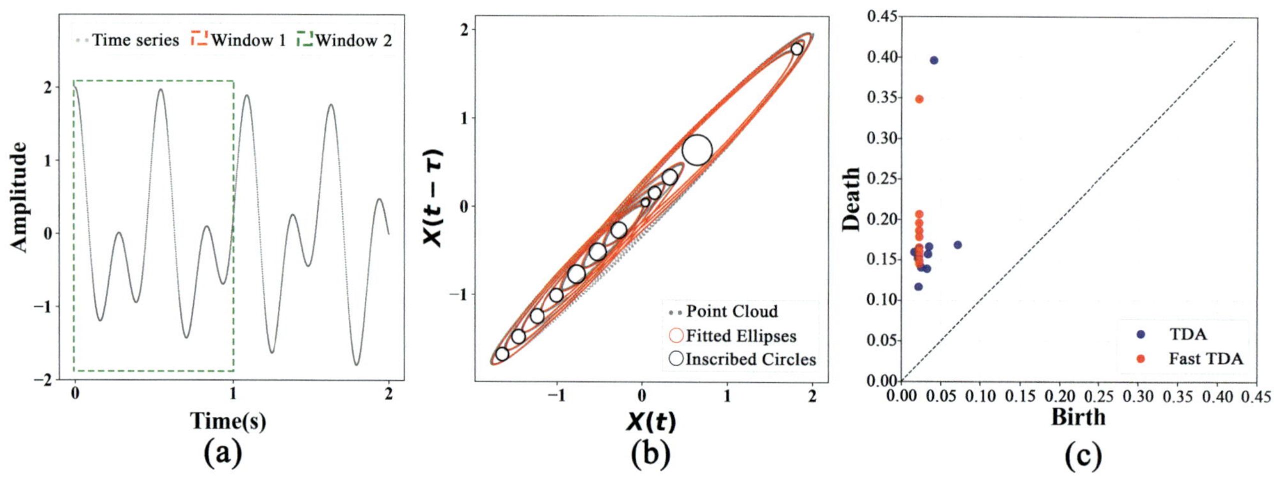

Fig. 5 TDA and Fast-TDA feature comparison for noise-free dual harmonic signal.

Figure 5 (b) and 6 (b) shows the fitted ellipses and inscribed circles, and Figure 5 (c) and 6 (c) compares the H_1 persistence diagram for the H_1 feature from TDA and Fast-TDA. For better comparison, the birth and death times for the first 10 points with longer persistence are listed in Tables 3 and 4. The results indicate that adding noise to the system causes a 60% change in the maximum persistence of H_1 from TDA but only a 1% change in the maximum persistence value from Fast-TDA. For points with shorter persistence, the changes are still significant in TDA compared to Fast-TDA. The number of off-diagonal points increases from 13 to 25 in TDA when moving from a noise-free to a noisy environment, whereas in Fast-TDA the number of off-diagonal points decreases from 11 to 10. Results show that adding noise to the system has a much smaller impact on the features extracted by Fast-TDA compared to TDA.

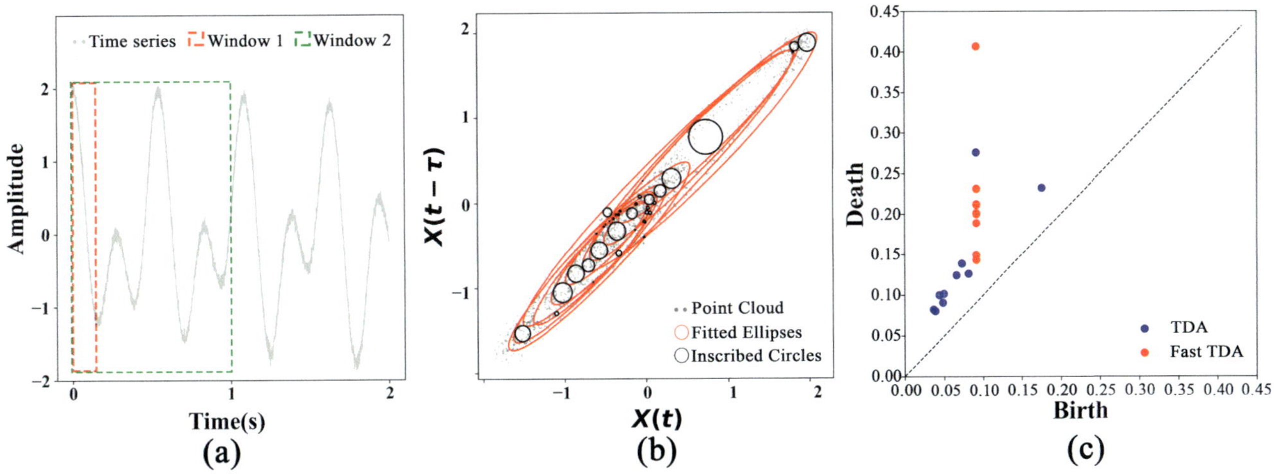

Fig. 6 TDA and Fast-TDA feature comparison in noisy dual harmonic signal.

Table 3 Birth and death values of the first 10 points using TDA and Fast-TDA for the noise-free dual harmonic signal

Method	Feature	Point 1	Point 2	Point 3	Point 4	Point 5	Point 6	Point 7	Point 8	Point 9	Point 10
TDA	Birth	0.040	0.016	0.022	0.020	0.035	0.033	0.024	0.032	0.071	0.021
(H_1)	Death	0.396	0.159	0.164	0.152	0.166	0.157	0.140	0.139	0.168	0.116
Fast-TDA	Birth	0.022	0.022	0.022	0.022	0.022	0.022	0.022	0.022	0.022	0.022
(Diameter)	Death	0.348	0.206	0.195	0.185	0.178	0.165	0.161	0.154	0.148	0.145

Table 4 Birth and death values of the first 10 points using TDA and Fast-TDA for the noisy dual harmonic signal.

Method	Feature	Point 1	Point 2	Point 3	Point 4	Point 5	Point 6	Point 7	Point 8	Point 9	Point 10
TDA	Birth	0.090	0.072	0.065	0.175	0.043	0.049	0.036	0.080	0.047	0.038
(H_1)	Death	0.275	0.138	0.124	0.232	0.099	0.101	0.082	0.126	0.090	0.080
Fast-TDA	Birth	0.090	0.090	0.090	0.090	0.090	0.090	0.090	0.090	0.090	0.090
(Diameter)	Death	0.406	0.231	0.230	0.212	0.211	0.201	0.199	0.188	0.149	0.143

Conclusion

In this paper, we propose the concept of *Fast-TDA* for noisy and chaotic signals, which estimates TDA features directly from a point cloud of data without necessitating the computation of filtrations or persistence diagrams. The development of the Fast-TDA approach was motivated by the deployment of TDA at the sub-millisecond realm, targeting applications to high-rate systems. The results showed that Fast-TDA could be a powerful method to extract topological features inspired by TDA, significantly improving computing time outperforming traditional TDA in a noisy and chaotic environment while being less sensitive to pre-TDA known hyperparameters (window size).

Acknowledgments The authors would like to acknowledge the financial support from the Defense Established Program to Stimulate Competitive Research (DEPSCoR) award number FA9550-22-1-0303, the Air Force Office of Scientific Research (AFOSR) award number FA9550-23-1-0033, and the National Science Foundation awards numbers CCF-1937460 and CCF-2234919. Any opinions, findings, conclusions, or recommendations expressed in this material are those of the authors and do not necessarily reflect the views of the sponsors/organizations, the United States Air Force, or the US government.

Disclosure of Interest

The authors declare that they have no known competing financial interests or personal relationships that could have appeared to influence the work reported in this paper.

References

1. Gowdridge, T., Dervilis, N., and Worden, K. "On topological data analysis for structural dynamics: an introduction to persistent homology". *ASME Open Journal of Engineering*, 1:011038 (2022)
2. Carlsson, G. "Topology and data". *Bulletin of the American Mathematical Society*, 46(2):255–308 (2009)
3. Carlsson, G. and Vejdemo-Johansson, M. *References*. Cambridge University Press (2021)
4. Takens, F. "Detecting strange attractors in turbulence". In *Lecture Notes in Mathematics*, pages 366–381. Springer Berlin Heidelberg (1981)
5. Alexander, Z. *A topology-based approach for nonlinear time series with applications in computer performance analysis*. PhD thesis, University of Colorado at Boulder (2012)
6. Kantz, H. and Schreiber, T. *Nonlinear Time Series Analysis*. Cambridge University Press (2003)
7. Stark, J. "Delay embeddings for forced systems. i. deterministic forcing". *Journal of Nonlinear Science*, 9:255–332 (1999)
8. Dlugas, H. "Electrocardiogram feature extraction and interval measurements using optimal representative cycles from persistent homology". *bioRxiv*, pages 2022–02 (2022)
9. Umeda, Y. "Time series classification via topological data analysis". *Information and Media Technologies*, 12:228–239 (2017)
10. Nelson, M., Barzegar, V., Laflamme, S., Hu, C., Downey, A.R., Bakos, J.D., Thelen, A., and Dodson, J. "Multi-step ahead state estimation with hybrid algorithm for high-rate dynamic systems". *Mechanical Systems and Signal Processing*, 182:109536 (2023)
11. Razmarashooli, A., Martinez, D.A.S., Chua, Y.K., Laflamme, S., and Hu, C. "Real-time state estimation using recurrent neural network and topological data analysis". In *Nondestructive Characterization and Monitoring of Advanced Materials, Aerospace, Civil Infrastructure, and Transportation XVIII*, volume 12950, pages 106–114. SPIE (2024)
12. Dodson, J., Downey, A., Laflamme, S., Todd, M.D., Moura, A.G., Wang, Y., Mao, Z., Avitabile, P., and Blasch, E. "High-rate structural health monitoring and prognostics: An overview". In *Data Science in Engineering, Volume 9: Proceedings of the 39th IMAC, A Conference and Exposition on Structural Dynamics 2021*, pages 213–217. Springer (2022)
13. Schrader, P.T. "Topological multimodal sensor data analytics for target recognition and information exploitation in contested environments". In *Signal Processing, Sensor/Information Fusion, and Target Recognition XXXII*, volume 12547, pages 114–143. SPIE (2023)
14. Aurenhammer, F. "Voronoi diagrams—a survey of a fundamental geometric data structure". *ACM Computing Surveys (CSUR)*, 23(3):345–405 (1991)
15. Nelson, M., Laflamme, S., Hu, C., Moura, A.G., Hong, J., Downey, A., Lander, P., Wang, Y., Blasch, E., and Dodson, J. "Generated datasets from dynamic reproduction of projectiles in ballistic environments for advanced research (DROPBEAR) testbed". *IOP SciNotes*, 3(4):044401 (2022)
16. Kausel, E. *Advanced Structural Dynamics*. Cambridge University Press (2017)
17. Small, M. *Applied nonlinear time series analysis: applications in physics, physiology and finance*, volume 52. World Scientific (2005)
18. Buzug, T. and Pfister, G. "Optimal delay time and embedding dimension for delay-time coordinates by analysis of the global static and local dynamical behavior of strange attractors". *Phys. Rev. A*, 45:7073–7084 (1992)
19. Downey, A., Hong, J., Dodson, J., Carroll, M., and Scheppegrell, J. "Dataset-2-dropbear-acceleration-vs-roller-displacement" (2020)

For Product Safety Concerns and Information please contact our EU representative GPSR@taylorandfrancis.com Taylor & Francis Verlag GmbH, Kaufingerstraße 24, 80331 München, Germany